PUTTING THE VICE IN
THE VICE-PRESIDENTS

PUTTING THE VICE IN VICE-PRESIDENT

Alan Naldrett

NEW NALDRETT PRESS

c) 2019 Alan Naldrett and New Naldrett Press

ISBN-10: 1091894181

ISBN-13: 978-1091894181

Alan Naldrett

Table of Contents

Introduction

Number One Observatory Circle, Washington, D.C. has been the Vice-President's residence since it was donated by Nelson Rockefeller in 1974.

INTRODUCTION

I always thought the best job anywhere would have to be Vice-President of the United States. You get free lodging in your own mansion (Number One Observatory Circle), free use of your own plane (Air Force Two), and plenty more perks, like good seats in restaurants, and lots of good swag. The only thing you ever had to do, assuming the President didn't die, was be President of the Senate. This mainly entailed sitting at a big desk in front of the assembled Senate, and not doing anything other than voting in a tie situation. Although most VPs used their position to direct proceedings, this was not a requirement. You could just sit there and read if you wanted.

The Vice-President even has his own song to march into, like the President has "Hail to the Chief." The Vice-President's song is "Hail Columbia."

But most people looked down on the Vice-Presidency for probably the same reasons a profligate like me would like it. Daniel Webster said when offered the Vice-Presidency, "I do not propose to be buried until I am dead." Thomas Jefferson said about the Vice-Presidency, "The second office of this government is honorable and easy, the first is but a splendid misery."

For those who thought the Vice-Presidency was a stepping-stone to the Presidency, Teddy Roosevelt said that the Vice-Presidency was a "stepping-stone to oblivion."

Many politicians considered the Vice-Presidency to be the kiss of political death. The lead Republicans at the beginning of the 20th Century wanted to limit Teddy Roosevelt's "progressive" influence in the party by getting him elected Vice-President. Thereby, in their estimation, this would render Teddy powerless. To their chagrin, President William McKinley was assassinated, making Teddy President.

So, the Vice-Presidency, in the words of FDR's first Vice-President

John Nance Garner, is considered by many to be "not worth a bucket of warm spit." This is chiefly because the Constitution did not specify duties for the Vice-President except to state that, in the case of the President's death, disability, or resignation, the "Powers and Duties of the said Office ... shall devolve on the Vice- President" (Article II, section 1).

Air Force Two in flight.

"Devolve" is defined as "to transfer or pass on to." This was vague, not saying whether the Vice- President became the President until a new election could be held, or whether he was to just assume the mantle of the President until the end of the four-year presidential term. This was solved fifty years later by John Tyler, the first Vice-President to ascend to the Presidency. Tyler became President in 1841 when President William Henry Harrison died a month into his term. When documents came to be signed by the "Acting President," Tyler simply crossed out "Acting," and became *the* President until the end of what would have been Harrison's term.

To make up for the disparity in duties for the Vice-President, Congress passed a law to make the Vice-President the President of the Senate. His two duties as President of the Senate were "to cast a vote in the event of a Senate deadlock, and to preside over and certify the official vote count of the U.S. Electoral College." And for this, the Vice-President is paid $230,700 per year, plus a $20,000 office allowance.

Despite the perceived anonymity of the job, many of the Vice-Presidents are well-known today, especially the ones who became President, such as Teddy Roosevelt and Harry Truman. There's Al Gore, who went on to become known for winning the Nobel Prize for his documentary on global warming, *A True and Present Danger.* Vice-President Charles Dawes also won a Nobel Prize in 1925 for a plan to lighten war reparations, and also wrote the tune which became a popular classic, *It's All in the Game.*

However, most people would not recognize the names of most Vice-Presidents. Levi Morton, Richard Johnson, and Daniel Tompkins are not "household names," as Spiro Agnew would say. Although there have been many volumes written about Vice-Presidents, they are usually known during their terms of office, thereafter, not so much.

A word on sources—some books on the Vice-Presidents are written seriously, some are not so serious. And then there are books like *Focus On: 40 Most Popular Vice-Presidents of the United States.* Which begs the question, how do you determine who were the most popular Vice-Presidents? Was there a poll I missed?

Unfortunately, the book doesn't list its criteria for making the list. Of course, I had to figure out which Vice-Presidents were not popular enough to make the list. Charles Curtis, George M. Dallas, Thomas Hendricks, Thomas Marshall, Levi Morton, James Sherman, Daniel Tompkins, and William A. Wheeler are the ones did not make the cut. They are the "Unpopular Vice-Presidents." Mike Pence wasn't around yet, so he didn't make the cut either.

Since there are many words already written on the most well-known VPs (VP—short for Vice-President), I have concentrated more on the ones who are not as well-known, including the Unpopular VPs. In the case of well-known VPs like Thomas Jefferson and John Adams, I've tried to concentrate on their Vice-Presidential terms. Good or bad, these are the stories of the Vice-Presidents of the United States!

Vice-Presidential Motorcade

JOHN ADAMS—HIS ROYAL ROTUNDITY, THE VICE-PRESIDENT

Everybody loved George Washington, and one of the main reasons was that he could have been King but was happy to serve only two terms as President. It wasn't easy being second-in-command to someone as popular as Washington, but John Adams (1735–1826) did his best. It wasn't until he became President himself that his troubles began.

Adams was born on October 20, 1735 in Braintree (since renamed Quincy), Massachusetts to a well-connected family. His great-great grandparents were John and Priscilla Alden, pilgrims who sailed over to the New World on the Mayflower. Adam's father John, whom he was named for, was a farmer, a leather craftsman, and a constable, selectman, and tax collector in his community, giving his son the impetus to enter public service.

Young Adams attended academies until entering Harvard at the age of 16. He graduated in four years with a Bachelor of Arts and then got a law degree. He was admitted to the bar in 1751, fifteen years before the American Revolutionary War, and began practicing law. He opened a law office in his home town of Braintree and had a successful practice.

In 1764 he married the well-read Abigail Smith and they had three sons and two daughters together. The marriage lasted 54 years—even though Adams would be gone for years at a time, with his public service. Abigail was one of the first women's rights advocate and would always gently remind her husband when he left for Washington to "look out for the women too John."

Early on, Adams opposed British taxation without representation, one of the main causes of the American Revolution. He led the opposition to the Stamp Act, and then, proclaiming that everybody deserved legal representation, defended the British soldiers of the Boston Massacre. He was a delegate to the First and Second Continental Congresses in 1774 and 1775 and signed the Declaration of Independence. He also helped negotiate the treaty ending the war with Britain and became Britain's first ambassador from the United States. He went on from there to represent the United States in France and the Netherlands.

With the introduction of the U.S. Constitution in 1788, George Washington was elected President, and, as the new Constitution stipulated, Adams was Vice-President because he got 34 Electoral Votes, the second highest. When Washington ran for a second term, both Washington and Adams were re-elected.

As Vice-President, he was a strong supporter of the Administration's programs. He often advised Washington although Washington didn't often listen—setting the tone for Vice-Presidents to follow. Adam's 29 tie-breaking votes in the Senate helped strengthen the federal government. Some sources, mostly those friendly to Adams, say Washington would often consult with him.

However, other accounts say Washington *didn't* consult with Adams much because, at the beginning of their terms, Adams got involved in a discussion on what to call the President. Although the eventual decision was "Mr. President," Adams felt the title should be more lofty-sounding and favored *His Highness*. Other Adams suggestions were *"His Majesty the President," "His Highness" "His High Mightiness,"* and *"His Mighty Benign Highness."* Washington was unhappy that so much time was spent on such a petty matter and blamed his Vice-President.

Because of Adam's tendency to lecture the Senate, he was not real popular. The nickname given Adams, *His Rotundity,* stuck for a long time. In turn, Adams remarked, "I have reached the conclusion that one useless man is called a disgrace, that two are called a law firm, and that three or more become a Congress."

When Washington decided not to run for another term, Adams

ran for President and won, becoming the second President of the United States.

By 1796, two major political parties arose. One was John Adam's and Alexander Hamilton's party, the *Federalists,* and the other was the *Democrat-Republican,* the party of Thomas Jefferson. Adams won the close election with 71 electoral votes, versus the 68 that Jefferson received.

For the first three years of his term, Adams stayed in the "Presidential Mansion" in Philadelphia. In the last year of his term, he and Abigail moved to the still-unfinished Executive Mansion, later called the White House. Abigail would use the East Room to hang her laundry.

Adams had struggles in his term, most notably with the *XYZ Affair,* dealing with French diplomats, and the *Alien and Sedition Acts* which limited freedom. Perhaps the most hated was the *Sedition Act,* which made "false, scandalous, and malicious writing" against the government or its officials a crime. These laws were very unpopular and led to decreased popularity for Adams.

More decreased popularity followed as Adams developed what was called an "imperious" attitude. In the next election, Adams lost to his political rival, Thomas Jefferson, and become the first one-term President. He retired to Massachusetts.

Ironically, he started a lively correspondence with Jefferson during their last years, and both died on the same day, the 50th anniversary of the Declaration of Independence, July 4, 1826. Adam's last words were "Thomas Jefferson still lives," although he had died only a few hours earlier. The man who had health problems all his life and started smoking when he was eight-years-old, lived to the hearty old age of 90.

He was the longest-lived President for many years until recently beat by several ex-presidents who have reached the age of 90. The record for oldest living President is now held by George H.W. Bush at 94, followed by Jimmy Carter, Gerald Ford, Ronald Reagan, and then Adams, followed by Herbert Hoover, who all lived into their 90s.

John Adams birthplace

Thomas Jefferson paintings by Mather Brown

THOMAS JEFFERSON– THE SMARTEST VEEP, WHICH PROBABLY ISN'T SAYING MUCH

John Adams might have had a few bad marks on his history—there was that Alien and Sedition Acts thing, and the pompous reputation, but his reputation did not get historically worse after he died (on the same July 4th as Adams). Unfortunately, for his Vice-President, Thomas Jefferson (1743-1826), the 2nd Vice-President and 3rd President, it did.

Jefferson's reputation suffered when it was scientifically established that he was the father of children of a woman, Sally Hemings, who was his slave, along with other indiscretions in his treatment of her (and his) family. To have sexual relations with someone who is unable to refuse has always been viewed as a reprehensible act.

Jefferson was born the third of ten children, on his father's tobacco plantation in what is now Albemarle County in Virginia. As the oldest son, Jefferson became the head of the family, at age 14, when his father died in 1757. At age 16 he entered the College of William and Mary and upon graduation in 1762 began to study law under a noted judge, George Wythe. In 1767 he was admitted to the Virginia bar.

In 1769 Jefferson briefly served as a Justice of the Peace before joining the Virginia legislature. He served there for five years, along with Patrick Henry and other Virginia freedom fighters. He married Martha

15

Wayles Skelton in 1772, having two daughters survive infancy. Martha died in 1782, and Jefferson never remarried.

In 1775 Jefferson joined the 2nd Continental Congress and wrote the Declaration of Independence (assisted somewhat by Ben Franklin, John Adams, Roger Sherman, and Robert Livingston). From 1775 to 1885, Jefferson served as Governor of Virginia, a member of the Virginia legislature (where he wrote the Virginia Charter of Religious Freedom), and a member of the U.S. Congress under the Articles of Confederation.

In 1785 Jefferson became Minister to France, taking Ben Franklin's place. After the U.S. Constitution was adopted, President George Washington appointed Thomas Jefferson as the first Secretary of State for the U.S. government.

Jefferson and Alexander Hamilton had opposite views of government, with Hamilton favoring a more autocratic way. With Hamilton the first Secretary of the Treasury, Jefferson had lots of opportunity to debate him and the first two political parties were formed. Hamilton headed the Federalist Party, which favored a strong federal government, and Jefferson was more in favor of state's rights in the Democratic-Republican Party, which eventually became just the Democratic Party.

Upon Washington's retirement both John Adams and Thomas Jefferson sought the Presidency. When Adams won, and Jefferson came in second, under the rules of the Constitution at the time Jefferson became Vice-President. Following his one-term as President, Jefferson again challenged Adams for the Presidency and won this time. Jefferson became the first President to be inaugurated at the White House.

Jefferson served two terms as President. Notable achievements included the Louisiana Purchase and sending the U.S. Marines to combat the Barbary Pirates.

After his second term Jefferson retired to his estate, Monticello, where he lived 17 more years, invented the swivel chair and dumbwaiter, and founded the University of Virginia. Jefferson never did think much of his Vice-Presidential reign, but then again, he didn't think much of his Presidential term either. The only things he wanted written on the tombstone he designed himself were "Author of the Declaration of Independence [and] of the Statute of Virginia for Religious Freedom & Father of the University of Virginia."

When he died on July 4, 1826 he was buried at Monticello.

A ARON BURR— DUELING FOR DOLLARS

Aaron Burr (1756-1805) was the 3rd Vice-President and probably the most infamous, since he killed the first Treasury Secretary and man pictured on the ten-dollar bill, Alexander Hamilton. Although Burr was reportedly a brilliant, witty and charismatic man, he was also an extravagant, self-centered, and treacherous mental deviant.

Aaron Burr's grandfather was famed minister Jonathan Edwards and his father Aaron, Sr., helped found Princeton University. Aaron, Jr. entered Princeton (then known as the College of New Jersey) at the age of 13 and graduated in 1772. In 1774 he began to study law and was licensed to practice law in New York in 1779. He spent a short stint in Washington's army during the Revolutionary War where his regiment fought and won the Battle of Monmouth in 1778.

Burr became involved in politics and was elected to the New York state legislature in 1784. Burr became attorney general of New York in 1789 and went on to be elected to the U.S. Senate. He served from 1791 to 1797 as part of the "Democratic-Republican" party that later morphed into the Democratic Party.

For the contentious election of 1800, each of the two major parties ran a slate with President and Vice-President. The Federalists, who favored a strong central government, ran John Adams and Charles Pinckney as their candidates. The Democrat-Republicans had Thomas

Jefferson and Aaron Burr. With each side bad-mouthed and used negative campaigning in a way not seen in previous elections.

Through a fluke in the election laws of the time, Jefferson and Burr each had the same number of electoral votes and the election had to be decided in the House of Representatives. With Alexander Hamilton's backing, Jefferson beat Burr and became President while Burr became Vice-President.

Burr kills Alexander Hamilton in a duel.

While he was still Vice-President, Burr ran for Governor of New York. Alexander Hamilton made derogatory remarks about Burr and Burr challenged him to a duel. Burr and Alexander Hamilton had been long-time political rivals when they faced each other on the dueling field July 11, 1804. Burr killed Hamilton with his shot, and then returned to Washington, D.C. (which had no extradition laws) and resumed his duties presiding over the Senate!

Burr lost the election for Governor of New York and was not re-nominated to run as Vice-President during Jefferson's second term; George Clinton got the nod instead. As he finished his VP term in 1805, the now unpopular Burr was already plotting how he could again attain power.

The crux of his plan, which would eventually get him arrested for treason, would have Burr inciting the Spanish possessions in Mexico, Latin America, and the Caribbean to revolt. From there a separate country would be formed, of which New Orleans would be the capital and Burr would be the man-in-charge.

One of his co-conspirators, James Wilkinson, spilled the beans on the plot and Burr was arrested. His trial was presided over by Supreme Court Chief Justice John Marshall. Burr was found not guilty since he had not yet started to foment the riot he had planned. This was in spite of the fact that it was revealed that Burr had told the British Ambassador that he would start a riot with Britain being the beneficiary if Britain paid him $110,000.

Burr fled to Europe where he had an audience with Napoleon and made roughly the same deal he had offered to the British. He eventually came back to the U.S. to see his daughter, who died in a shipwreck before they could reunite.

After that, Burr remained in the U.S. and once again successfully practiced law in New York. He died at the age of eighty and was buried in Princeton, New Jersey. He apparently never paid for his "crimes." On the day he died, his marriage to his current wife was officially terminated on the grounds of adultery. Burr included two illegitimate children in his will.

Alan Naldrett

G EORGE CLINTON— NOT THE FUNK SINGER

George Clinton (1739-1812) was from Ulster County, in New York, where he was born on July 20, 1739. At first a farmer, he studied law and passed the bar in 1764. In 1768 he was elected to the New York State Assembly, which then met at Kingston, New York.

In those Pre-Revolution days, Clinton often voted with the Tories, which is what they called British sympathizers. But his mind changed as the British passed the *Quartering Act*, allowing British soldiers to be quartered in American homes, and the *Townsend Act*, taxing stamps, tea, and other items. This angered Clinton enough to join the Revolution!

In 1770, Clinton married Cornelia Tappen and lived in Ulster County. He was elected to the Second Continental Congress in 1775. During the American Revolution he was a Brigadier General and successfully defended Ulster, Westchester, Duchess, and Orange Counties, as well as the highlands of the Hudson River.

In 1777, he was elected the first provincial Governor of New York, and he continued as Governor of New York for the next 18 years. A major education advocate, he was instrumental in getting New York State University erected.

He retired to his farm in 1793, but when Cornelia died in 1800, he accepted the Vice- President position during Jefferson's second term, replacing the exiled Aaron Burr. He was unfortunately considered less skillful than Burr at moving things along in the Senate. He was forgetful and didn't pay close attention to details. He often

Clinton, though widely regarded as senile, declared his intention to run for President in 1808. So, when James Madison followed Jefferson as President in 1808, he kept Clinton on as Vice-President, causing Clinton to be the first Vice-President to serve under two different Presidents.

However, Clinton was not placated by being given the Vice-Presidential nod once again. He resented Madison because Clinton thought that *he* should be President. When it was Clinton's turn to break a tie regarding the Bank of the United States charter that Madison wanted to renew, Clinton voted against it.

Clinton was in ill health through much of his term with Madison, and died at the age of 73 in Washington, eleven months before his term was up. He was the first Vice-President to die while in office. He was not replaced, since there was no provision at that time for replacing a Vice-President who had become disabled, died, or resigned while in office.

Vice-President George Clinton's Grave Memorial at the Old Dutch Churchyard in Kingston, New York.

It's unfortunate that most people, when they hear the name George Clinton, either think of the funk musician with the same name or think he's a cousin of Hillary and Bill.

Not the Vice-President George Clinton.

ELBRIDGE GERRY —THE FATHER OF GERRYMANDERING

It is not many people who are responsible for a word to be created out of their name, but Elbridge Gerry (is most remembered for "gerrymandering," a word that denotes setting boundaries in an election district to favor your candidate. The one-time Massachusetts governor's map was said to look like a salamander, so the combination of Gerry and salamander came to be gerrymander. However, Gerry's surname is pronounced with a hard "G," as in "give," while gerrymandering is pronounced with a soft "g," like "generous."

Elbridge Gerry was born in 1744 in Marblehead, Maryland. He was educated by private tutor and entered Harvard when he was 14, earning a B.A. in 1762 and an M.A. in 1765. He entered his father's merchant/shipping business and became wealthy.

Elbridge Gerry birthplace in Marblehead, Massachusetts

When the British blocked off Boston Harbor, Gerry transported goods from Marblehead to the colonists on his families' ships. He was a member of the first and second provincial congresses of 1774-1776 and later served in the Continental Congress that was the forerunner of Congress before the Constitution was adopted, as well as signing the Declaration of Independence. He was also in the Massachusetts legislature.

Gerry was described as someone who distrusted the "common man" and felt that he shouldn't be trusted with the vote. He was also a bit of a prude and wanted Ben Franklin recalled from France due to his infidelities. He also wanted to ban stage plays in Massachusetts. John Adams said that he "opposed everything that he did not propose."

While in France, due to being appointed to a three-man commission to investigate the XYZ Affair, his other two commissioners left. Gerry stayed, saying that maybe he could come up with a solution on his own. Sure enough, when he came back the U.S., he proclaimed that he prevented war with France, even though no further details were ever forthcoming.

Gerry ran for Governor of Massachusetts four years in a row, 1801-1803. The Massachusetts gubernatorial term was for only one year. He tried again in 1810 and was successful. He won re-election once, and then was defeated again.

Gerry applauded the War of 1812, saying, "We have been at peace too long, a good war will help us."

When his VP George Clinton died nine months before his first term was over, Madison needed a Vice-President for his second term. He asked Gerry, and despite frail health, Gerry accepted the Vice-Presidential position. He became the fifth Vice-President in 1813.

Unfortuneatly, Gerry became the second Vice-President in a row to die during his term—Gerry died of a lung hemorrhage during an evening carriage ride. So far President Madison is the only President to have two Vice-Presidents die during his tenure.

The Boston Gazette, in their March 26, 1812 issue, first used the term "gerry-mandering."

Gerry's gravesite in Centennial Cemetery in Washington, D.C.

DANIEL D. TOMPKINS.

DANIEL D. TOMPKINS
—ALCOHOL ALLOWED

The sixth Vice-President, Daniel D. Tompkins (1774-1825), was also the fourth Governor of New York. He was born in Scarsdale, New York in 1774, earned a law degree at Columbia College, and then practiced law in New York City. He went on to the New York Supreme Court, after which he was elected Governor of New York, a position he held for ten years. Tompkins was known as an abolitionist, and a spokesperson for humane treatment of Native Americans.

During the War of 1812, Tompkins patriotically raised money for the armed forces, going so far as to put thousands of his own money in the war pot. He didn't keep good records and said that the cause was too important to worry about the accounting now, and that it would "all be sorted out later." This would come back to haunt him later.

In 1816 Tompkins made a good showing in the Presidential race, coming in second behind James Monroe. Monroe then asked Tompkins to be his Vice-President. When Monroe ran again in 1820, he kept Tompkins for his running-mate and together they won another four-year term. Unlike his two predecessors, Gerry and Clinton, Tompkins lived out his term, but passed away just 99 days after serving as VP, at the age of 50. He *was* the first VP to serve two full terms since John Adams.

Tompkins ran for Governor of New York while still Vice-President but lost to De Witt Clinton, the man who was the patron of the Erie Canal and former VP George Clinton's nephew. Also occurring during the eight-year term was the issuing of the Monroe Doctrine, and the Missouri Compromise. A lack of rancor caused the period to be called "The Era of Good Feeling."

It may have been an era of good feeling for most, but for Tompkins it was more about feeling good. He had many problems that he tried to cure with alcohol. The problems included going broke. By the time of his second Vice-Presidential term, he was inebriated most of the time, spending little time at his President of the Senate duties. President Monroe called him a "troubled soul." His Vice-Presidential salary of $5,000 per year was garnished by

Tompkins' drinking was also exasperated by the accusations he had mis-appropriated $120,000 while he was head of the New York War Effort during the War of 1812. He spent most of his eight years as VP trying to clear his name. He was present as President of the Senate during James Monroe's first term, but mostly absent during the second term, so much so that the Senate had to appoint a permanent President Pro Tempore.

Everyone thought that Tompkins, a youthful 42 when he became VP, would be a welcome change after having the two previous, older Vice-Presidents die before completing their terms. And Tompkins did become the first Veep since John Adams to serve two complete terms. But ironically, he just barely made it, dying just 99 days after his term was over. He was buried in Saint Mark's Church-In-The-Bowery in Manhattan,

New York.

Many years after his death, the books were properly balanced, and it was discovered that Tompkins did not owe <u>anything</u>. He was actually <u>owed</u> a few thousand dollars, and this was paid to his descendants.

Daniel Tompkins Memorial in Scarsdale, New York

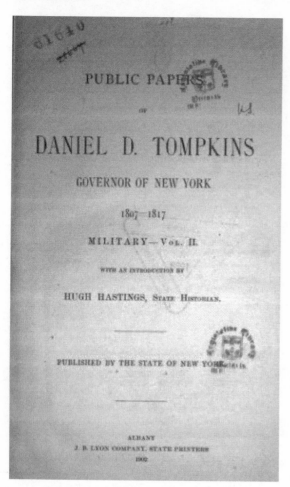

PUBLIC PAPERS

OF

DANIEL D. TOMPKINS

GOVERNOR OF NEW YORK

1807—1817

MILITARY—VOL. II.

WITH AN INTRODUCTION BY

HUGH HASTINGS, STATE HISTORIAN.

PUBLISHED BY THE STATE OF NEW YORK

ALBANY
J. B. LYON COMPANY, STATE PRINTERS
1902

Gravesite of Daniel D. Tompkins at St. Mark's Church-In-The-Bowery, Manhattan, NY, NY

Alan Naldrett

JOHN C. CALHOUN —TWO PRESIDENTS, ONE RESIGNATION

John C. Calhoun (1782-1850) and George Clinton were the only VPs to ever serve under two different presidents. Calhoun was also the first Vice-President to resign. He was known as a fiery legislator from the South.

Calhoun attended school in Georgia and then went to Yale University in 1802. He graduated in 1804 with a law degree and was admitted to the South Carolina Bar. He opened a law office in Abbeville in 1807 and then in 1808, won a seat in the South Carolina State Legislature. In 1811 he was elected to the U.S. House of Representatives.

John   C.   Calhoun

birthplace

The next year was when the War of 1812 started, and Calhoun was one of the "War Hawks" that helped push the U.S. to war with Great Britain. During his three terms in the House he chaired the Foreign Relations Committee. In 1817, he became the Secretary of War under President James Monroe.

In 1924, Calhoun threw his hat into the Presidential race. When it was clear that his party, the Democrat-Republicans, were leaning towards John Quincy Adams or Andrew Jackson, he set his sights on the Vice-Presidency, hoping to use that office as a Presidential stepping stone.

He took seriously his President of the Senate duties, using his position to undermine his now political rival, President John Q. Adams. He cast the most tie-breaking votes in the Senate of any other Vice-President—31. Adams and Calhoun would vent their anger towards each other by writing letters about the other to the newspaper, using pseudonyms.

Calhoun survived a scandal during his first VP term. He was accused of benefiting from a defense contract awarded to his assistant's family. Although found blameless, he nevertheless suffered a blow to his popularity.

By 1828 the antipathy between President Adams and his VP Calhoun came to a head when in 1828 Calhoun threw his support behind Andrew Jackson for President. In return, Jackson added Calhoun to his ticket as Vice-President. Adams added Richard Rush of Pennsylvania to his ticket but was handily defeated by the Jackson/Calhoun ticket.

Calhoun soon ran afoul of his new President in 1829. In a dispute dubbed the "Petticoat Affair," Jackson was mad when the Secretary of War's wife Peggy Eaton was shunned by the other Cabinet wives. This was due to supposed impropriety Peggy had with John Eaton while her husband was lost at sea (even though he was later reported dead). The shunning made Jackson mad because his late wife had also been subject to the practice. When most of the wives refused to stop the shunning and welcome Peggy Eaton to their tea parties (their leader was Calhoun's wife Floride), most of Jackson's Cabinet, including Calhoun near the end of his term, turned in their resignations.

Jackson also learned that Calhoun had wanted to have Jackson court-martialed during the War of 1812 for not following orders. Jackson later remarked that one of his big regrets as President was not having the power to have Calhoun hanged.

Calhoun's resignation came at a period when he was a big advocate for state's rights and the state's rights to veto or nullify a program they didn't agree with. Jackson was vehemently opposed to nullification, as the practice was known. When Calhoun's feelings that state's rights trumped federal laws became known, his Presidential star was no longer rising. Nevertheless, he returned to the Senate when he was appointed to a vacant South Carolina Senate seat in 1932. He kept the seat until his death in 1850, except for a short stint from 1844 to 1845 as President John Tyler's Secretary of State. He was the founder and leader of the short-lived, states-rights Nullifier Party.

Calhoun in his later years was known as a slavery and state's rights advocate, a position for which he was celebrated in the South. There are many counties, cities, and other municipalities named for him.

Confederate bill with Calhoun

Monument to Calhoun in Charleston, SC

Alan Naldrett

MARTIN VAN BUREN—VP TURNED HAND-PICKED SUCCESSOR

Martin Van Buren (1782-) was from Kinderhook, New York where his father owned a tavern. He went to Kinderhook Academy and at the age of 14 began to study law. He trained in a New York City law office and was admitted to the New York Bar in 1803. In 1807 he became counselor of the New York Supreme Court and in 1812 was elected to the New York State Senate. In 1816 he was appointed attorney general of New York State and became one of the party leaders for the Democratic-Republican Party.

In 1820 he was elected to the U.S. Senate. Upon re-election in 1826, he served for two years and then resigned when he was elected Governor of New York in 1828. Upon Jackson's win as President in 1929, Van Buren was appointed Secretary of State. This was a new job every year for three years.

During the "Petticoat Affair," Van Buren curried favor with President Jackson when he was one of the few who would visit with the shunned Peggy Eaton.

Free Soil Party poster

In 1832 Jackson was looking for a Vice-Presidential replacement for Calhoun, who had resigned during Jackson's first term. He selected Van Buren as his running mate for the upcoming election and Van Buren accepted. The Jackson/Van Buren team handily defeated the opposition led by Henry Clay of the National Republican Party (which morphed into the Whig Party), and his running mate, John Sergeant of Pennsylvania. Other political parties making an appearance in this first election year, that had conventions to nominate candidates were the Nullifier Party and the Anti-Masonic Party.

Van Buren proved to be a loyal Vice-President to Jackson, promoting Jackson's policies in the Senate. When Jackson retired after two terms, he appointed Van Buren his successor. With Richard Johnson as his Vice-President, Van Buren won the Election of 1836. Van Buren was the third Vice-President (after John Adams and Thomas Jefferson) to win his own term as President.

Unfortunately, his term fell within the Panic of 1837, when the country went into a major recession. He was blamed and dubbed "Martin Van Ruin."   Other nicknames for Van Buren were "The Little Magician" and "The Fox." These were due to his short height (5 foot and 6 inches) and what were thought to be his tricky, sly ways.

Van Buren's home in Kinderhook, New York.

Van Buren lost re-election in 1840 and Whig President William Henry Harrison and his VP John Tyler took over the White House. Van Buren was the third sitting President to win re-election. (The other two were John Adams and John Quincy Adams.)

After being President, Van Buren campaigned for the Democratic nomination again in 1844 but lost out to Speaker of the House James K. Polk. In 1848 Van Buren unsuccessfully ran for President again as the candidate for the Free-Soil Party.

Van Buren retired to his birthplace, Kinderhook, New York, and was buried there, after living to be 82 years old.

RICHARD M. JOHNSON— RUMPSEY DUMPSEY DUMPED AS VP

Richard Mentor Johnson (1781-1850) had the ignominious honor of being the first Vice-President to be tossed from a Presidential ticket. This, and other actions, (such as not even carrying his home state of Kentucky in the Presidential election) helped Richard Johnson make most of the other VPs look good in comparison. He was one of three Johnsons to be Vice-President (the others were Andrew and Lyndon) and the only one to not become President.

A frontier man in the style of Andrew Jackson, he was born in 1780 in the new settlement of "Beargrass" Kentucky, later to be renamed Louisville. He studied law at Transylvania University and was admitted to the Kentucky bar in 1802. He helped build roads with Daniel Boone, and then got elected to the Kentucky House of Representatives.

In the *Battle of the Thames* in the War of 1812, he let an exaggeration of his role in the death of Indian Chief Tecumseh go unchallenged. The account was that he sent his troops on their way while he was injured and when they came back, they reported that Tecumseh had been killed during the night. Johnson took credit, and when running for Vice-President, used the slogan, "Rumpsey Dumpsey, Rumpsey Dumpsey, Colonel Johnson killed Tecumseh."

From 1819 to 1829, Johnson represented Kentucky in the Senate. Andrew Jackson was the patriarch of the Democratic Party and his chosen successor as President was his Vice-President Martin Van Buren.

Since another of the Jackson supporters was Johnson, he was chosen to back up the ticket as Vice-President in 1837.

However, this was back when Presidents and Vice-Presidents were elected separately (even if they ran as a team) and Martin Van Buren was elected, but Johnson did not receive a majority. He was the first (and to date, only) Vice-President that had to be elected in the Senate. He was the seventh Vice-President.

The more people found out about Richard Johnson, the less they liked him, especially since it was the pre-Civil War era when slavery was allowed. Not only did Johnson possess slaves but entered a common-law marriage with his slave Julia Chinn and had two children. He publicly acknowledged his wife and children, saying, "Unlike Jefferson, Clay, Poindexter and others I married my wife under the eyes of God, and apparently He has found no objections." The men he mentioned were all rumored to have had relations with their slaves. When Julia died of cholera in 1833, he was deeply grieved.

However, despite Johnson's admonitions and trying to get his daughters into "polite society," he still did not include them in his will, his estate going to his surviving brothers John and Henry. Once Julia died, he began a relationship with another of his slaves. When she left him for another man, he had her hunted down and sold at auction. He then began a relationship with her sister. Johnson also owned a tavern, a fact which was objectionable to many people. He was also said to be a "non-bather."

As President of the Senate, Johnson was considered one of the worst, He would often get up and walk around, chat with anyone within sight, and be inattentive when he did sit in his President of the Senate chair. This was when he showed up, because he would leave to tend his tavern, even when the Senate was in session, for up to nine months at a time.

Johnson tried to convince the Senate that the United States should be the first country to drill a hole to the center of the Earth, and, because he liked getting mail, he thought that the mail should be delivered seven days a week.

He became so unpopular that Martin Van Buren dropped him from the ticket (the first time that ever happened) and did not officially have a running mate since the Democratic Convention refused to endorse

Johnson for a second term. This is to date the only time a Presidential candidate ran without a Vice-President. But this didn't stop Johnson for running for Vice-President on his own, making him one of the few to actively pursue the position.

Johnson hurt the ticket more when he would show up to campaign stops inebriated, and launch into an incoherent, rambling speech. Remarks he said about opponent William Henry Harrison touched off a riot in Cleveland, Ohio.

Van Buren was spared the embarrassment of a Vice-President he didn't want when the team lost to Harrison and John Tyler. Johnson petitioned to become President in 1844 but was largely ignored. He finally made a successful return to the public life when he was elected to the Kentucky House of Representatives. However, he died *two weeks* into his term.

Two of his main achievements are getting debtor's prisons banned, and the first college, *Choctaw Academy,* for Native Americans. He was interred in the Frankfort Cemetery, in the state capital of Frankfort, Kentucky.

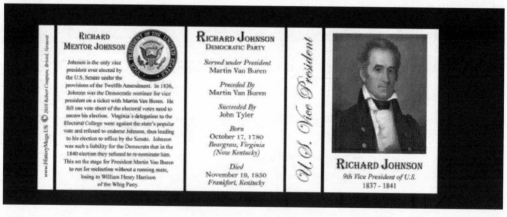

Burial site of Richard M. Johnson, Frankfort Cemetery, Kentucky

Alan Naldrett

JOHN TYLER-HIS ACCIDENCY

The greatest achievement of John Tyler (17?-1852) might have been transforming a President's role when becoming President upon the death of a President from "Acting President" to just plain "President." This is because of what happened upon the death of William Henry Harrison, the first President to die in office. Harrison succumbed to pneumonia 30 days after his inauguration, after giving a three-hour inaugural address in the cold without a hat or overcoat.

According to the Constitution, the Vice-President, John Tyler, was to assume the duties of the President. As correspondence came for Tyler to sign, the notation under where he was to sign identified him as "Acting President." Tyler crossed out the "Acting" portion. This set the precedent that the Vice-President became the President.

Tyler was born in Charles City County, Virginia in 1790 to aristocratic parents. He graduated from William and Mary College, was admitted to the bar in 1810, and in 1811 was elected to the Virginia House of Delegates in 1811. At the age of 26 in 1816, he was elected to the U.S. House of Representatives. In 1825 he became Governor of Virginia. He resigned to join the U.S. Senate, then resigned the Senate in 1836.

By the 1840 Presidential election, Tyler was a seasoned politician. He consented to be the Vice-President to William Henry Harrison's President and was the Tyler in the political slogan, "Tippecanoe and Tyler Too." They had no platform to speak of, just log cabin homilies about Harrison, even though he actually grew up in a mansion.

The Harrison-Tyler duo beat the incumbent Democrat, Martin Van Buren. They were the first Whigs to be elected, with Tyler being only one of two Whig Vice-Presidents (Millard Fillmore was the other).

There was not too much to speak of when it comes to Tyler's Vice-Presidential administration, since it was only one month. His Presidential administration was contentious, with Tyler vetoing much of his own party's legislation. He was also pro-slavery, which went against Whig sentiments. One of the many unfortunate quotes about him was spoken by Teddy Roosevelt when he said Tyler was "a politician of monumental littleness."

It was not all bad. During his administration, the Weather Bureau was established, the U.S. Navy was organized, the Seminole War was ended, the Orient was opened to U.S. trade, and Florida and Texas were admitted to the Union.

However, Tyler was such a contrarian about following the Whig Party platform that he was expelled from the party in 1841. Tyler then finished his term without a party.

John Tyler birthplace in Charles City County, Virginia.

At the end of his term in 1845, Tyler went back to Virginia and practiced law. He tried to use whatever influence he had at that point to preserve the Union, but then when Virginia seceded with the Southern states, he was elected to the Confederate House of Representatives. His death in 1862 occurred before the House met and Tyler could take his seat.

He was buried in Hollywood Cemetery, in Richmond, Virginia. Not overly popular because of the Confederate thing, it wasn't until 1911 that Congress voted that a monument be erected.

John Tyler gravesite in Hollywood Cemetery in Richmond, Virginia.

GEORGE M. DALLAS —THE BIG D

In 1792, George M. Dallas (1792-1864) was born in Philadelphia to Arabella and James Dallas. James Dallas was a former Secretary of the Treasury under President James Madison and was briefly Secretary of War. At first John Dallas' son George had an auspicious beginning, graduating with honors, earning a law degree from the College of New Jersey (later Princeton).

Dallas was admitted to the Pennsylvania bar in 1813 and worked at federal appointments including "remitter of the Treasury" until 1820, when he became the Deputy District Attorney for Philadelphia. He went on an appointment as Minister to Russia. In Russia he asked to come home because "there isn't anything happening here."

He was elected Mayor of Philadelphia (as the candidate of the "Family Party") and left that post in 1829 to become the United States attorney for the eastern district of Pennsylvania. In 1831, he won a special election to fill the U.S. Senate post left vacant by Isaac Barnard's resignation. When that term was complete in 1833, he spent two years as the Pennsylvania Attorney General.

In 1837, he returned to Russia as the Minister to Russia until 1839, attempting to conclude the Russian border line problems.

At the Democratic Convention of 1844, unpopular President Martin Van Buren couldn't get a 2/3 majority in his own party to be nominated for another term. After nine ballots it was decided the candidate would be dark horse, former Tennessee Governor and one-time Speaker of the House James K. Polk, who promised to run for only one term. The Vice-Presidency was offered to Senator Silas Wright of New York

The new-fangled telegraph was just starting to be widely used and the offer was telegraphed to Wright. He sent back a one-word reply: "NO." Wright refused because he had supported Van Buren. Not believing that anyone would outright refuse such a prize as the Vice-Presidency, on a silver platter, the offer was again sent to Wright. His indignant reply was: FIND...SOMEONE...ELSE...STOP.

The position was then offered to Dallas, who accepted after being awakened in the middle of the night. The team of Polk and Dallas beat the Whig ticket of Henry Clay and Theodore Frelinghuysen. The Whig's slogan was "The Country's Risin' for Clay and Frelinghuysen."

V.P. Dallas was consulted by President Polk, and performed his President of the Senate duties well, casting 19 tie-breaking votes in just four years. One of his tie-breaking votes was for an unpopular tariff, which got him burned in effigy in Philadelphia.

Polk did as he promised and did not run for a second term. Dallas was mentioned as a candidate but was offered and accepted the position of Minister to the Court of St. James in London, England. He stayed there, with his family, for four years, returning in 1861.

Returning to Philadelphia, he returned to private life as President of the Atlantic and Great Western Railroad, until his death in 1864, due to a heart attack. He was 72. Dallas County in Texas was named in his honor.

MILLARD FILLMORE —VEEP, PRESIDENT, KNOW-NOTHING

Millard Fillmore (1800-1875) was the twelfth Vice-President and thirteenth President. He was elected in 1848 with fellow member of the Whig Party, General Zachary Taylor, hero of the Mexican War, as President. Fillmore had one of the shortest VP terms, serving just until 1850, when he became President upon Taylor's premature death. Taylor was at a fund-raising event for the Washington Monument and succumbed to a form of "Asiatic Cholera" after drinking iced milk and raw fruit.

Fillmore grew up poor in the Finger Lakes section of New York where his parents were tenant farmers. Without a lot of formal schooling, he scraped together enough money and did enough self-studying to pass the New York bar. He maintained a successful law practice in the Buffalo area and was elected to the New York Assembly in 1828. In 1835, he was elected to the U.S. House of Representatives.

Fillmore was a man of many political parties, starting in the National Republican Party, and then joining the Anti-Masonic Party. This was a party that started off opposing Masons (and secret societies in general), and then added a few more planks to their platform. Fillmore was able to work himself up to a position of strength in the party. But by the 1830s, most of the members, including Fillmore, joined the Whig Party. One of his accomplishments during this period was leading the fray to get debtor's prisons banned in New York State.

Fillmore ran for Governor of New York in 1844 but was narrowly defeated by Democrat Silas Wright. He returned to his successful private practice for a few more years and then was elected New York Comptroller in 1847.

In 1848, the Whigs nominated Zachary Taylor for President and tapped Fillmore to fill the number two position to run against the Democratic team of Michigan's Lewis Cass and Kentucky's William O. Butler. Taylor was from Virginia and a slaveholder so Fillmore, a New Yorker and non-slave holder, was brought in to balance the ticket. Also running was eighth President Martin Van Buren on the Free-Soil Party ticket. Van Buren's running mate was Charles Adams, son of sixth President John Quincy Adams.

The Free-Soilers only managed to garner 10% of the vote and no electoral votes. The Taylor/Fillmore team won with 47% of the vote.

As Vice-President, Fillmore was not consulted by Taylor on the issues of the day, which mostly consisted of antagonism between slavery states and non-slavery states. Fillmore knew that Taylor's Cabinet was probably all very pro-slavery. So, once he became President, he dismissed them and replaced them with his own choices, including making his old law partner, Nathan K. Hall, the Postmaster General, which was then a Cabinet-level position.

With his new Administration, Fillmore signed the Compromise of 1850 into law, a compromise measure to hold off secession by the Southern states. This measure included the controversial Fugitive Slave Act, and Fillmore's popularity dwindled greatly once it started being enforced.

In fact, Fillmore was so unpopular by the Election of 1852 that his own party did not nominate him for a second term, the second time this had happened to a Whig. (Whig John Tyler was also President when the Whigs refused to renominate him.) Fillmore was both the last Whig President and Vice-President. During his term, Japan was opened to trade by the U.S. Navy, California became a state, and Fillmore appointed Brigham Young as Governor of Utah. After his term, many Whigs joined the Republican Party.

But Fillmore wasn't done changing parties either. When the Know-Nothing Party (also known as the American Party), an anti-Catholic, anti-immigrant party, nominated Fillmore for President in 1856, he accepted the nomination. He came in third but garnered 21% of the vote, one of the best third-party performances in U.S. election history.

After this, he retired from public life. When his wife Abigail died in 1873 (she started the first White House library), he married a wealthy widow, Caroline McIntosh. For the rest of his life, he and his wife devoted their lives to philanthropy and entertaining. Fillmore died of a stroke in 1874 and was buried in Buffalo.

Alan Naldrett

ZACHARY TAYLOR,
WHIG CANDIDATE FOR PRESIDENT.

MILLARD FILLMORE,
WHIG CANDIDATE FOR VICE PRESIDENT.

Alan Naldrett

WILLIAM RUFUS KING— FIRST CLOSETED VICE-PRESIDENT

William Rufus King (1786-1853) was the fourth Vice-President to die in office. He died 45 days after his term began. This was still not the shortest VP term, as John Tyler and Andrew Johnson both served less upon becoming President due to the deaths of William Henry Harrison and Abe Lincoln.

During the election campaign, King had been in ill health with tuberculosis and had gone to Havana, Cuba, hoping the climate would help him. Congress gave permission to swear him in there in Cuba. But he soon realized his days were numbered and he returned to his native Alabama where he died two days later. He is to date the only person from Alabama to be Vice-President.

William King was born in North Carolina in 1786 to a well-to-do family. He went to the University of North Carolina in Chapel Hill and joined the North Carolina bar in 1806. In 1807 he was elected to the North Carolina House of Commons and served there until 1809. He became the city solicitor of Fayetteville, North Carolina in 1810, and from 1811 until 1816 he was in the U.S. House of Representatives.

King went to Russia in 1816 as assistant to the Minister to Russia. He returned in 1818 to buy land in Alabama and start a large cotton-growing operation, which utilized slave labor. Along with the rest of his family, King owned over *500* slaves.

William Rufus King estate

King was a delegate to the convention which organized the State of Alabama in 1819. When Alabama was admitted to the Union as the 22nd state, King was chosen to represent Alabama in the U.S. Senate. He served in the Senate until 1844. From 1844 to 1846 he served as Minister to France.

Returning to the Senate, in 1850 he was named President Pro Tempore of the Senate due to Zachary Taylor's death. Finally, in 1852 he was named as Vice-President on the Democratic ticket with Franklin Pierce as President. The Pierce-King ticket defeated the Whig ticket of Winfield Scott and William Alexander Graham.

When King died just weeks into his term, he was buried in Selma, Alabama, a city he named for the Ossianic poem, *The Songs of Selma*.

King might best be remembered for his relationship with future President James Buchanan, who he lived with for 13 years, from 1840 until his death in 1853. They had planned to run for President and Vice-President as a team. They did all the social functions in Washington together and were referred to as the "Siamese Twins." Andrew Jackson referred to them as "Miss Nancy" and "Aunt Fancy."

William King had a county named for him in Oregon in 1852. However, the honor was rescinded when the county voted to declare that King County was thereafter named for Martin Luther King.

William King's crypt in Selma, Alabama

Alan Naldrett

JOHN C. BRECKENRIDGE-
CHOSE THE WRONG SIDE

John Cabell Breckenridge (1821-1875) had it all he was a handsome, intelligent, and charismatic man from a prominent Kentucky family. His grandfather was John Breckenridge, a Senator from Kentucky and Attorney General in Thomas Jefferson's Cabinet. His childhood friend was Mary Todd Lincoln. He passed the bar at the age of 20, was a leader in the Kentucky legislature by 28, and the youngest Vice-President ever, elected at the age of 35 and 36 when he assumed office.

In 1845, Breckenridge established a successful law practice in Lexington, Kentucky. In 1846, he was given a commission of Major during the Mexican War. He was elected to the Kentucky State Legislature in 1849, and in 1851 was elected to the U.S. House of Representatives, where he served two terms.

In 1856, the Democratic Convention nominated James Buchanan for President and Breckenridge for Vice-President, an office Buchanan looked down on and had twice refused. The duo beat the brand-new Republican Party, with Presidential candidate John C. Fremont and Vice-Presidential candidate Walter Drayton, 174 to 114 electoral votes. He was the 14th Vice-President and served from 1857 until 1861.

Once he was elected to the second-highest office in the land, in typical Vice-Presidential fashion, it all went downhill from there. The U.S. had just completed four years with Franklin Pierce, who mostly drowned his sorrows over his son's death instead of trying to alleviate the imminent storm clouds brewing over the nation due to the slavery issue—the

South wanted to keep slavery, the North wanted to outlaw it.

As Breckenridge began his Vice-Presidential term, he conducted his President of the Senate duties well. However, the few times he was consulted by President Buchanan made Breckenridge doubt Buchanan's ability to handle the Presidency. One time, Buchanan asked his VP if he thought the nation would respond and end their animosities if he declared a "Day of Humiliation and Prayer."

As Vice-President Breckenridge tried to work with fellow Democrats to prevent the Civil War and the dissolution of the Union. But as the situation worsened, the Election of 1860 was hotly disputed. There were four candidates, each preventing the others from getting a majority. The Democratic Party split, with a candidate from the North, Stephen Douglas, and V.P. Breckenridge, for the Southern Democrats. Still another was John Bell of the new Constitutional Union Party.

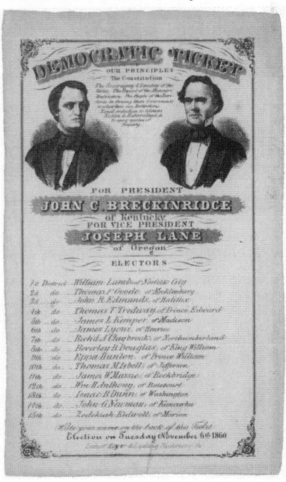

Breckenridge's running mate was the Senator of Oregon, Joseph Lane. Lane started in the Indiana Legislature and was appointed to be the Governor of the Oregon Territory by President James K. Polk. When Oregon achieved statehood, Lane was elected the first Senator. He consented to be Breckenridge's running mate in 1860. This effectively ended Lane's political career, since the Southern Democratic Party supported slavery.

The winner in 1860, with 40% of the vote, was the Republican candidate, Abraham Lincoln, and his running mate Hannibal Hamlin. Breckenridge and Lane came in second.

Breckenridge was also in favor of slavery. He had been elected Senator of Kentucky and remained neutral until Kentucky was invaded by the Union. Breckenridge chose to go with the South and was made a Brigadier General for the Confederate Army. He was also declared a traitor by the Union Army.

After the 1862 Battle of Shiloh, Breckenridge was promoted to Major General in the Confederate Army. He fought against the Union at the Battles of Murfreesboro, Chickamauga, Vicksburg, Chattanooga, and Cold Harbor. In February 1865, President of the Confederacy Jefferson Davis appointed Breckenridge his Secretary of War.

When the Confederacy lost the Civil War, Breckenridge was still wanted on a treason charge and went on the run. He was the second Vice-President to be accused of treason, but unlike Aaron Burr, he was never brought to trial. On the run for three years, he made stops in Cuba and different countries in Europe.

Finally, a general amnesty was declared, and Breckenridge returned to Lexington and resumed practicing law. He continued until he died at the age of 54 due to a liver ailment. His wife Mary lived until the age of 81 and the couple had six children together.

Breckenridge was not the only former U.S. Vice President to join the Confederate government. John Tyler was elected to the Confederate House of Representatives but died before he could begin his term.

The gravestone of John C. Breckenridge doesn't mention his Vice-Presidency.

Alan Naldrett

HANNIBAL HAMLIN— VICE-PRESIDENT AND MAINE COAST GUARD MEMBER

Hannibal Hamlin (1809-1891) was a staunch abolitionist from Maine. He was born in Paris, Massachusetts (now in Maine) in 1809 and at first managed his father's farm, and then became a newspaper editor. He studied law and was admitted to the Maine Bar in 1833.

He opened a law office in Hampden, Maine, and then started his political career in the Maine Assembly. He went on to the U.S. House of Representatives and then to the Senate. He then ran for Governor of Maine, won, and then resigned after six weeks to go back to the Senate. In the meantime, he supported every anti-slavery bit of legislation. Due to his abolitionist views, he changed political parties from the Democratic to the Republican Party in 1856.

Probably not believing that the ticket could win but wanting to show that he supported the party, Hamlin agreed to run as Vice-President under Lincoln. Running on the Republican ticket, they were among the four parties to run candidates in the 1860 election.

The reason for so many candidates was that the Democratic Party split into Northern and Southern factions and each one had their own candidate. Candidate John C. Breckenridge (the former VP) ran for the Southern Democrats with Joseph Lane as VP and took 18.1% of the vote. Stephen Douglas, with VP candidate Herschel Johnson, ran for the Northern Democrats and won 29.5% of the vote. John Bell and famed orator Edward Everitt ran for the Constitutional Union Party and got 12.6% of the vote. So, to Hannibal's surprise, the Republicans received 39.8% of the vote, and won the election!

Hamlin went on to call the Vice-Presidency "the most unimportant office, neglected by the president, the cabinet and Congress." Despite his disdain for the office, he did manage to get a few key projects through, including the entry of blacks into the military.

He did not stay around Washington much after being elected. Most of the time he left his President of the Senate duties to a President Pro Tempore and went to his Maine farm to do chores. He even signed up for a stint for the Maine Coast Guard during his Vice-Presidential term!

One of the few times Hamlin presided over the Senate, he had a drunken Senator expelled, causing a rule to be passed banning liquor in the Senate chambers.

Despite his public aversion to the office, Hamlin was still surprised when he was bypassed by Lincoln when it came time for re-election. Instead, Andrew Johnson of Tennessee, a border state, was selected over Hamlin.

Hamlin was elected to the Senate again, and later served as ambassador to Spain. He was the third Vice-President to die on July the 4th (in 1891) after John Adams and Thomas Jefferson.

ANDREW JOHNSON— FIRST IN IMPEACHMENT

Andrew Johnson (1808-1875) had a rough time of it as both Vice-President and the 17th President. Following an icon like Abraham Lincoln wouldn't be easy, but Johnson also had the distinction of becoming President following the Civil War and during the difficult Reconstruction years.

He grew up poor because his porter father died when he was two, leaving his mother to support three kids as a seamstress. Johnson was apprenticed to a tailor when he was 13. After two years he skipped out of the rest of his apprenticeship and opened his own tailor business in Laurens, South Carolina.

In 1826 Johnson moved with his mother, brother, and stepfather to Greenville, Kentucky where he opened a larger tailor shop. It was here that he met and married Eliza McCardle and had five children with her. Johnson was not the most well-read President—he didn't learn to read until Eliza taught him when he was in his twenties.

He was elected to the Greenville Town Council in 1826, and after serving three terms he became Greenville's Mayor. From there he was elected to the State Legislature in 1834 and served in both Tennessee Legislative branches until 1843, when he was elected to the U.S. House of Representatives. In 1853 he was elected Governor of Tennessee. He was re-elected in 1854 and then elected to the U.S. Senate in 1857. When Tennessee seceded from the Union, he refused to follow suit.

Abraham Lincoln wanted a new running-mate for the 1864 election and chose Johnson since he was a loyal Unionist and was from a border state. The Republicans changed their name for this election to the "National Union Party," a name the Republicans chose to lure voters from border states and to get War Democrats and others that wouldn't vote for a "Republican" party. Winning the election, Johnson did not impress a lot of people when he showed up drunk to his inauguration. He was less than two months into his Vice-Presidential term when President Lincoln was assassinated, making Johnson President.

Andrew Johnson birthplace in Raleigh, North Carolina, before restoral.

Andrew Johnson birthplace, restored.

89

Johnson had one of the most difficult Presidencies of anyone. He wished to follow Lincoln's lead on Reconstruction and not punish the South for losing the Civil War. But Congress was of another mind and seemed to want to punish Johnson for thinking differently. The House of Representatives impeached Johnson for doing something that was his right as President—replacing a Cabinet member. There weren't enough votes in the Senate to expel him as President and he finished out his term, not running for re-election.

For a long time after, Johnson did not hold any public offices. Finally, in 1874 he was elected to the U.S. Senate from Tennessee, the only ex-President to date to become a Senator after being President. (John Quincy Adams was elected to the House of Representatives after his Presidency.)

Johnson didn't live to finish out his Senate term; he had a stroke and died two days later, in 1875.

S CHUYLER COLFAX-RAILROADED IN RAILROAD SCANDAL

Schuyler Colfax (1823-1885) was born in New York City in 1823 and attended elementary school there. His father died before he was born, and his mother remarried. The family moved from New York to New Carlisle, Indiana when he was 13. His first job was as a clerk in the post office and then he moved on to helping his stepfather as Deputy Auditor for St. Joseph County. The family moved to South Bend, Indiana for the position.

Colfax studied law but never passed the bar. He instead started a newspaper that had Whig sentiments, the *St. Joseph Valley Register,* in 1845. He was on-board for Indiana's state Constitutional Convention in 1850 and was on ground zero when the Whigs morphed into the Republican Party. He supported the Republican anti-slavery stance.

In 1854, he was nominated and won a seat in the U.S. House of Representatives as a Republican. He was re-elected six times and became Speaker of the House in 1863, a position he kept until his election as the 17th U.S. Vice-President in 1869.

In 1868, Colfax ran for Vice-President with General Ulysses S Grant for President and the two of them won, defeating the Democratic ticket of Horatio Seymour and Francis P. Blair, Jr. He conducted his Vice-Presidential duties admirably and looked at the office as a stepping stone. When he was sure that Grant wouldn't pursue another term (Grant changed his mind), Colfax announced that he was a candidate for President in 1872 and would not seek another Vice-Presidential term.

However, this was before the Crédit Mobilier of America scandal. Politicians were discovered to have accepted cash bribes to facilitate Crédit Mobilier to charge higher prices than normal while building the Union Pacific Railroad. Implicated in the scandal were Colfax, and Henry Wilson, who was the man Grant chose for his running mate after Colfax announced his non-candidacy. Future Presidential candidate and Speaker of the House James G. Blaine, and future President James Garfield were also involved, but mostly unaffected by the scandal.

The scandal, while explained away by some of the other politicians, caused Colfax to end his Presidential aspirations. He thereafter continued publishing newspapers and became a celebrated speaker, having over 150 speaking engagements per year.

It was while he was on his way to a speaking engagement when he died in Mankato, Minnesota in 1873, at the age of 61. He was switching trains and had to walk over ¾ of a mile in -30 below zero (Fahrenheit) weather. This brought on a fatal heart attack. He was buried in South Bend, Indiana.

HENRY WILSON
Vice President of the United States

Born in Farmington February 16, 1812, Jeremiah Jones Colbath, this self-educated farm boy changed his name when of age to Henry Wilson. He became a teacher, member of Congress, United States Senator and took office as Vice President under President Ulysses S. Grant March 4, 1873. He suffered a stroke and died in the Vice President's chambers in the Capitol, November 22, 1875.

Alan Naldrett

HENRY WILSON— INDENTURED SERVANT, COBBLER, AND VICE-PRESIDENT

Since Henry Wilson (1812-1875), the 18th Vice-President, is not exactly a household name, one can't help but wonder if he wouldn't be more well-known if he had gone by his birth name, Jeremiah Jones Colbath. He was born to a poor couple near Farmington, New Hampshire in 1812. His birth father was a bigger fan of whiskey than he was of children, so young Jeremiah did not get much of an education. He was a big fan of books, though and read whatever he could get his hands on. He was indentured out to a farmer at the age of ten.

At the age of 21 Jeremiah legally changed his name to Henry Wilson, a person he had once read a biography about. He took the livestock he was given for earnings, sold the animals for $84, and then made the 100-mile walk to Natick, Massachusetts.

In 1833, the newly-christened Henry Wilson briefly apprenticed to a cobbler and then opened his own cobbler shop. He worked the shop and by 1839 had a successful shoe business with a factory and 18 employees. By 1846, the factory had grown to 52 employees. If that sounds like a Horatio Alger story, maybe that's because Horatio Alger was also associated with Natick, Massachusetts.

Wilson went on from his successful shoe business to the Massa-chusetts legislature, and served there from 1841 to 1852. He had a failed run for Governor, and then he went on to the U.S. Senate in 1854, where he served 18 years. His two main platforms were the abolition of slavery and improving working conditions for factory employees.

Henry Wilson's Cobbler shop

He was a Brigadier General during the Civil War and after the war caused over 300 KKK members to be indicted for crimes. He had started as a member of the Whig Party, but became disenchanted with their slavery platform, helped form the Free-Soil Party, which combined with the Democrats, had a brief flirtation with the anti-slavery American "Know-Nothing Party," and then became a Republican.

President Grant had to find a running mate for the 1872 contest, having lost Schuyler Colfax, his previous running mate, to Colfax's own Presidential ambitions and involvement in the Credit Mobilier railroad scandal. Wilson also had discounted Credit Mobilier railroad stock in his wife's name but returned it and escaped major trouble.

Wilson had referred to the Slave period as the "Slave Power" and wrote a lengthy, two-volume work on the history of slavery in the United States, *The History of the Rise and Fall of the Slave Power in America*. It was published, although unfinished, after his death.

Grant tapped Wilson to be his running mate and they won the 1872 contest. Unfortunately, Wilson suffered a stroke in 1873, three months into his term, and malingered until 1875, when he became the fourth Vice-President to die in office.

WILLIAM ALMON WHEELER—HE LOST THE POPULAR VOTE BUT WAS STILL A WINNER

William Wheeler (1819-1887) was the running mate of Rutherford B. Hayes, and the 19th Vice-President, serving from 1877 to 1881. He was born poor in 1819, in the "Northern Country" town of Malone in Franklin County, New York but managed to attend Franklin Academy and finish at the University of Vermont. He was admitted to the New York bar by the age of 21 and became the Malone Town Clerk and Superintendent of Schools. In 1846 he became the Franklin County District Attorney.

Wheeler went from the D.A.'s office to the New York State Assembly in 1849, as a Whig from the dwindling Whig Party. He served two terms and refused a third, returning to Malone to practice law and accumulate some money. This was although he refused to accept a pay raise while in the State Assembly. Wheeler became known for his honesty and strong moral fiber.

Birthplace of William Wheeler

Wheeler didn't stay away from politics long, returning as a New York State Senator in 1857. He quit the Whigs and came back as a member of the Republican Party. In 1860, he became a Republican U.S. Congressman from Northern New York.

When Wheeler served as President of the New York State Constitutional Convention in 1867, he came to national attention and became the running mate of Rutherford B. Hayes in the 1876 election.

The good news was that Hayes and Wheeler were declared the winners. The bad news was that it was the most contested election up to that date. The Democrats, led by incumbent Samuel Tilden, won the popular vote and perhaps the Electoral College. The votes of three Southern states were disputed and an election committee was formed. The committee voted along party lines, which made Hayes President, with an agreement to the Democrats to end Reconstruction.

With this unpromising beginning, Wheeler went on to have an unremarkable and non-controversial VP term, working as President of the Senate, and breaking a few ties. He was on good terms with President Hayes and was one of the few who would come to visit teetotalers Rutherford and Mrs. Hayes, the famed "Lemonade Lucy." Each time Wheeler would go to Lucy's lemonade parties, Hayes would remark how fond the family was of him. Perhaps it was because Bill Wheeler was lonely, having just lost his wife, Mary King Wheeler.

When Hayes decided not to pursue a second term in 1880, Wheeler followed suit and retired to Malone. He died in 1887 and was buried next to his wife in Malone's Morningside Cemetery. His June 30th birthday is celebrated annually by the Malone Historical Society.

CHESTER A. ARTHUR— KIND OF A CON

Chester Alan Arthur (1829-1886) was probably the most fastidiously-dressed President ever. Just upon being elected Vice-President, he went out and spent $700 (about $15,000 today) on clothes. Each month he would spend today's equivalent of $250.00 just on hats. He would change clothes several times during the day, and almost always wore a tux to dinner. Although he refused to have a bodyguard, he *did* employ a valet. Therefore, he was called the "Dude President," "Elegant Arthur," and the "Gentleman Boss."

JAMES A. GARFIELD
REPUBLICAN CANDIDATE FOR PRESIDENT

CHESTER A. ARTHUR
REPUBLICAN CANDIDATE FOR VICE PRESIDENT

Library of Congress

Arthur was just as fastidious with his living quarters—he had the whole White House remodeled and put off moving into it for three months until he was satisfied with it. He hired Louis Comfort Tiffany to head the restoration and spent the equivalent of $2 million dollars in today's money. He spent most of it on paintings, mirrors, new mantels, lighting fixtures, and stained glass while discarding over $400,000 in china, mantels, mattresses, and cuspidors.

Chester A. Arthur was born in Fairfield, Vermont (near the Canadian border) in 1829 and this became a subject of controversy later. His opponents claimed he was born on the Canadian side of the border, making him ineligible to be Vice-President or President.

Arthur's father was a Baptist minister and changed churches every few years, hence Arthur attended many different public schools. He graduated from Union College in 1848 and taught school for five years while he studied law. He was admitted to the New York bar in 1854 and began a law practice in New York City.

As a member of the Pulver and Clark Law firm, he championed African-American rights, and defended blacks in many incidents, including the one that led to the integration of New York trains.

In 1856, he joined the Republican Party and moved up in Republican circles, coming under the auspices of Boss Roscoe Conkling and his group known as "Stalwarts," who were the dominant political machine of the time.

In 1860, he was rewarded for his party loyalty by being appointed by New York Governor Edward D. Morgan as the State Engineer-in-Chief. The appointment carried with it a military rank of Brigadier General. During the Civil War Arthur served as Quartermaster General and Inspector General of the New York Militia.

Chester Arthur was appointed by President Grant to the lucrative position of Collector of the Port of New York in 1871. It was lucrative because it had long been the custom to award the collector who discovered pirated goods a percentage of the recovery. This system was called "moiety" and allowed Arthur to make many times his $12,000 annual salary. In fact, this particular perk of the job allowed Arthur a take-home pay of $40,000-$50,000 per year, a rich salary for the 1870's.

Arthur was dismissed from his Collector of the Port position by President Rutherford Hayes, in Haye's crusade to reform the "spoils system." The spoils system allowed each winning political party to appoint all *their* constituents to the best and most important Civil Service posts.

Boss Conkling wanted more control in Presidential politics and less Civil Service reforms. He was insulted when he was only given the opportunity to have one of his Stalwarts as Vice-President instead of having more say in deciding who would be President. James Garfield had as one of his platforms the reform of the Civil Service to eliminate the spoils system. Conkling was against any change to the profitable system he had helped set up.

Conkling thought he was just being appeased when his fellow Stalwart Levi Morton was offered the Vice-Presidency, so he had Morton politely decline the VP position. However, Arthur was not so inclined. When the convention then went to Arthur with the Vice-Presidential offer, Arthur accepted against Conkling's wishes. However, when Conkling saw the consequences of the decision, which was Arthur becoming President, he was not averse to helping select Levi Morton as V.P. in 1889.

The consequences were that the ticket of James A. Garfield and Chester A. Arthur won the Presidential race of 1880. However, Garfield was only President for 199 days before he was shot by Charles Guiteau, a disgruntled civil service worker, who felt he should have been given a better position in Garfield's administration.

Guiteau had been planning the murder and stalking Garfield for a while. He even meticulously researched guns, selecting a .44 Webley British Bulldog model because he thought it would look good in a museum after the assassination. He made sure his shoes were top-grade because of all the attention he knew he'd get.

Garfield died of the gunshot wound and the subsequent vain attempts to find the bullet discharged within him. The assassination was on July 2, 1881, and Garfield spent two months being probed by doctors with non-sterile instruments before succumbing to both the gunshot wound *and* infection on September 19, 1881.

With Garfield's death, Arthur became President. Garfield's assassin had shouted out, "I am a Stalwart! Now Arthur is President!" To soothe feelings, Arthur severed all ties with the Stalwarts, even going so far as to investigate a post office scandal in which many Stalwarts were implicated.

One thing he didn't change was the spoils system, which had been one of the main platforms of Garfield's administration. Instead, his accomplishments as President include building up the U.S. Navy and reducing the national debt.

Once his term was over, Arthur did not attempt to run again. He had been diagnosed with Bright's Disease and went back to his law practice. He became head of the railway company building the New York subways.

In 1886, Arthur retired altogether after his Bright's Disease worsened in February. He died later that year on November 17, 1886 and was buried in Albany. On his deathbed, he told his son to burn all his Collector of the Port files.

T HOMAS HENDRICKS— ONLY BELIEVED WHITE PEOPLE TO EQUAL TO HIM

Thomas Hendricks (1819-1895) was the fifth Vice-President to die in office. Fortunately for him, that might be what most people remember about him, because he had a questionable career prior to becoming the

21st Vice-President. He openly opposed the 13th, 14th, and 15th Amendments, the ones that grant freedom, citizenship, and voting rights to African-Americans. A couple of quotes of his was, "This is the white man's government, made by the white man, for the white man" and that the black man "was inferior and no good would come from his freedom."

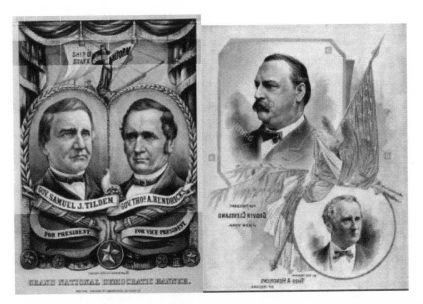

Hendricks was born in a log cabin in Zanesville, Ohio and in true Vice-Presidential style, moved to the number one state for Vice-Presidents, Indiana, in the village of Shelbyville. He went to Hanover College, studied law and was accepted to the bar in Indiana.

After opening a law practice in Shelbyville, he started his political career in 1851 by getting elected to the Indiana Assembly. In 1855 he moved on to the U.S. House of Representatives, and then in 1863 served a six-year term in the U.S. Senate. From 1873 to 1877 he was Governor of Indiana. He didn't attach great significance to his time as Governor, saying that "anyone competent enough to be a notary public could do be Governor of Indiana.

Hendricks was known as the "Professional Candidate" as he put his name in the running for President or Vice-President four times. A fellow Indiana Senator, Oliver P. Morton, said that his thirty years of non-achievement in office must have set some sort of record.

Hendricks first successful nomination as a Vice-Presidential candidate was as the running mate of Samuel Tilden, who won the popular vote in 1876 but controversially lost the election to Rutherford B. Hayes and William Wheeler in the Electoral College.

In 1884, the Republicans nominated Grover Cleveland for President, and once again, Hendricks for Vice-President. This time, the ticket won. Unfortunately, (for him), he only served until November 1885 when he died in his sleep. He was the fifth Vice-President to die while in office.

LEVI MORTON— INVESTMENT BANKER, COTTON BROKER, AND VICE-PRESIDENT

Levi P. Morton (1824-1920) started his business career long before his political career. He was born in Shoreham Vermont, in 1824, and his first job was as a clerk in a store in Hanover, New Hampshire. After working in Boston for an import business, by 1855 he owned his own wholesale business in New York City.

Morton suffered a big setback during the Civil War when he could not collect from all the Southerners who owed him money, but he made a comeback. In 1863 started a banking firm, Morton, Bliss & Company, on Wall Street that became one of the most successful in the U.S.

Morton was successful at investment banking, cotton brokering, and his wholesale business. He acquired a large fortune and in 1876 decided to try his hand at politics. He ran for the House of Representatives from the wealthy 11th District of New York City. He lost his first election but won a seat two years later in 1878.

In 1880 Morton was offered the Vice-Presidency under James Garfield. He refused and missed his chance to become President when James Garfield was assassinated less than a year into his term. Instead, Morton became Minister to France, which was the job that Garfield's assassin wanted and killed Garfield in revenge for not giving him.

Morton had been re-elected to the House in 1880 but resigned when Garfield appointed him Minister to France. He warmed to the ambassadorship, living in splendor and throwing lots of parties. While in France, he officially accepted the French gift of the Statue of Liberty and drove the first rivet into the statue in 1884.

Upon his return to the U.S., he made two tries to be elected to the Senate in 1885 and 1887 but lost both times. So, when Benjamin Harrison came calling with the offer to be his Vice President in 1888, Morton didn't refuse.

For the election, Morton did what he did best—raised money. Although they lost the popular vote by 10,000, they won the Electoral College vote 233 to 168, beating the incumbent President, Grover Cleveland.

Morton presided over the Senate as Vice-President. At one point, the Democrats were conducting a filibuster which Morton refused to end since he didn't agree with the Republican's position. This angered the

Republican administration, and in 1892 Morton wasn't offered the Vice-Presidential position again even though he was willing to take it. The Republicans instead chose New Yorker Whitelaw Reid.

However, Grover Cleveland won the election, the only person to serve non-consecutive Presidential terms. On the other hand, Levi Morton ran for Governor of New York and won in 1895. He again wouldn't follow party politics and lost party favor again. He was hoping to be nominated for President in 1896, but William McKinley got the nod instead. When Morton's New York Governor term ended, he quit politics to manage his businesses.

He formed the Morton Trust Company in 1899 and merged it with the Guaranty Trust in 1909. He spent his retirement traveling and living at his 1,000-acre estate in Rhinebeck, New York.

His first wife Lucy Young Kimball died in 1871. In 1873 he married Anna Livingston Street and the couple had five daughters. Anna died in 1918 and Levi died two years later, in 1920. Morton lived to be 96 and was the longest-lived Vice-President after John Nance Garner.

A DLAI STEVENSON —NOT THE GUY WHO LOST TWICE TO EISENHOWER

You would think that only one person would ever have the first name "Adlai," however, the Stevenson family has named four sons Adlai so far. The first is the one we'll examine, as he was the 23rd Vice-President. The second was the two-time Democratic candidate and former Illinois Governor, the third was a U.S. Congressman, and Adlai IV is a renowned journalist.

Getting back to the first Adlai Stevenson (1824-1920), he was born in Christian County in Kentucky in 1835. The original family came from Scotland, moved to Ireland, and then Pennsylvania, and finally, to North Carolina. Adlai's father John took his inheritance from *his* father's vast North Carolina estate and moved to Kentucky where Adlai was born. John then set his few slaves free and moved to Bloomington, Illinois, where he began to operate a sawmill.

Young Adlai attended from Illinois Wesleyan College in Blooming-ton, and Centre College in Kentucky, earning a law degree and joining the Illinois Bar in 1858, at age 23. During the Civil War he served a court civil appointment and in 1864 was a District Attorney. In 1875 he was elected to the House of Representatives and served from 1875 to 1877, and 1879 to 1881, representing Illinois. Besides the Democratic Party, he was also the candidate for the Independent Reform Party in the 1875 election, and for the Greenback Party in the 1879 election.

Stevenson became the U.S. Assistant Postmaster General from 1885 to 1889 and took this unlikely stepping-stone to become Grover Cleveland's running mate, in Cleveland's return to the White House. The slogan was "Cleve and Steve." Perhaps the quick promotion to VP candidate was because Stevenson had been Cleveland's "hatchet man" in the Post Office, firing over 40,000 Republicans and acquiring the nicknames "The Headsman" and "The Axe Man."

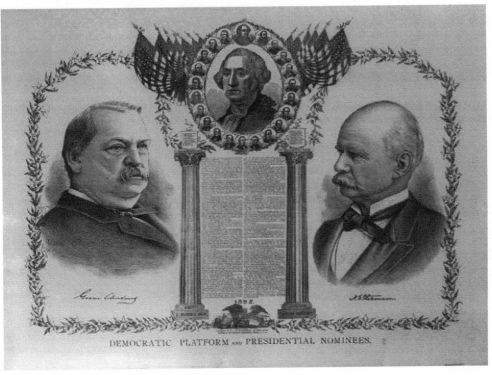

DEMOCRATIC PLATFORM and PRESIDENTIAL NOMINEES.

Cleveland-Stevenson campaign poster of 1892

The incumbent President Benjamin Harrison had just lost his wife and his zest for campaigning for another term. The election had a third-party, the People's Party, also called the Populist Party, which garnered 22 electoral votes.

Stevenson served as Vice-President for one term, from 1893 until 1897. He served with honor, well-liked and dutiful as the President of the Senate. However, it did not appear that he was consulted by President Cleveland very often. Stevenson was asked if Cleveland had ever consulted with him and Stevenson replied, "Not yet, but there are a few weeks of my term remaining."

With the usual load of work that a Vice-President had to do, which was basically nothing, Vice-President Stevenson took a train trip to Tacoma, Washington. There was a local battle on what to call the mountain that was the centerpiece of Tacoma. One side favored the old name, Rainier, and the town of Tacoma and the Northern Pacific Railway favored "Mt. Tacoma."

Stevenson realized he would make a lot of enemies, whichever side he chose when asked. So, not wanting to start any trouble, as Stevenson was speaking, he referred to the "beauty and majesty" of the mountain without calling it by name. Finally, at the end of his speech he said, "This controversy must be settled, and settled right now by the national government. I will not rest until this glorious mountain is properly named..." and at this point he arranged to have the train whistle blow.

Stevenson was back politically in 1900, as the running mate of William Jennings Bryan. But Bryan and Stevenson lost the election to Republicans William McKinley and his VP Teddy Roosevelt. Teddy would become President upon McKinley's assassination.

Stevenson went back into private law practice in Illinois, before making one last attempt at public office, running for Illinois Governor in 1908. At the age of 73, he narrowly lost.

He died in Chicago at the age of 78. He was interred in the family plot in Bloomington, Illinois. Besides his famous grandson namesake, he was also the great grand-uncle of McLean Stevenson, who played Col. Blake on the M.A.S.H. TV show.

Alan Naldrett

GARRET HOBART —VICE- PRESIDENCY AS A HOBBY

Garret Hobart (1844-1899) was born in Long Branch, New Jersey in 1844. Aaron Burr was born in New Jersey, but his career played out in New York and Washington, DC, so it's safe to say that Hobart was the only New Jersey Vice-President, since he lived and died there too, in Paterson.

Another Vice-President like Levi Morton who was primarily a businessman, Hobart attended Rutgers and graduated with honors in 1863. After a brief teaching career, he moved to Paterson, New Jersey and passed the bar in 1869.

His business enterprises included his law practice in New Jersey, serving as Director for many corporations, President of a few banks and insurance companies, and the Paterson Water Company and the Passaic Water Company. Hobart was said to consider his political career as just a hobby and concentrated his energies on his businesses. This helped him to amass a small fortune. His estate is still the centerpiece of Paterson.

Hobart started his political career in 1871 with a term on the Paterson City Council. He moved on to the State Assembly in 1872 and became the state Speaker of the House at age thirty in 1874. He then ran for the State Senate and served two 3-year terms.

Hobart started to know national political figures as he became chairman of the state Republican committee from 1880 to 1891 and a member of the Republican National Committee in 1884.

In 1896, the Republicans were confident they could recapture the White House after Grover Cleveland's second term included major national economic and labor troubles. The Republicans supported the gold standard and wanted someone to back up the Presidential ticket that was also a gold supporter. That someone turned out to be Hobart, who backed up William McKinley in the Presidential race of 1896.

Hobart Manor in Paterson, NJ

The team won against famed orator William Jennings Bryan who ran as the candidate for two different political parties, each with a different Vice-President candidate. Bryan's main party was the Democratic Party, which chose his VP running mate to be Arthur Sewall. (The other party that nominated Bryan was the Populist Party, which nominated Thomas Watson as its V.P. candidate.) McKinley was confident enough to do all his campaigning from his front-porch in Canton, Ohio.

Hobart had a successful Vice-Presidential run, performing his duties as President of the Senate admirably and becoming a trusted advisor to President McKinley. Hobart and his wife Jennie Tuttle (who he married in 1896) threw lots of parties in their rented mansion near the White House.

McKinley, who admired Hobart for his business acumen, often consulted his VP on various matters. So much that Hobart was dubbed the "Assistant President." Hobart was in on all the planning for the Spanish-American War, which occurred during McKinley's administration.

Sadly, Hobart became ill in the spring of 1899, and died in November, becoming the sixth Vice-President to die in office. His wife Jennie wrote two books, *Memories* and *Second Lady* before she died in 1941 at the age of 91.

Alan Naldrett

THEODORE ROOSEVELT —BIG STICK AND BULLY PULPIT

One of the most famous Vice-Presidents was Theodore "Teddy" Roosevelt (1858-1919), and one of the two men who were Vice-President to be on Mt. Rushmore. (Thomas Jefferson was the other.) Roosevelt was a good example of the heights a Vice-President could reach when he took over the Presidency, which he did upon the assassination of President William McKinley. Teddy parlayed the chance into becoming one of the most notable Presidents.

Roosevelt had a privileged upbringing, attending prestigious schools and making many trips abroad with his wealthy banker/merchant father Theodore, Sr. Offsetting this was Roosevelt's unhealthy childhood, afflicted with asthma and other illnesses. However, vigorous physical exercise helped him become healthy and robust by the time he was an adult.

Roosevelt entered Harvard in 1876 and graduated with honors in 1880. He then went to Columbia Law School and studied law but dropped out before getting a degree. In 1881, he was elected to the New York State Legislature as a Republican at the age of 23.

While in the State Legislature he fought crime and corruption in the state government. He was re-elected but quit when his wife Alice and his mother died on the same day on February 14, 1884. He assuaged his grief by traveling to the Dakota Territory in 1884 to 1886, managing a cattle ranch and serving as sheriff.

In 1886 he returned to New York, got remarried to Edith Carow, and unsuccessfully ran for mayor of New York City. He wrote books about the West (he wrote about 40 in his lifetime) before being appointed a civil service commissioner and serving from 1889 until 1895. From 1895 to 1897 he was the Police Commissioner of New York City.

In 1897 McKinley appointed Roosevelt his Assistant Secretary of the Navy. But Roosevelt overstepped his authority when he ordered General Dewey to attack the Spanish fleet in Manila Bay. He was fired but Roosevelt went to Cuba with his Rough Riders in the Spanish-American War, capturing Sagamore Hill and cementing a national reputation. He ran for Governor of New York in 1898 and won.

It was reported that when McKinley for President again in 1900, the party wanted Teddy where he couldn't get into trouble. Supposedly this is why they selected him for Vice-President, little knowing McKinley's 1901 assassination would make him President.

Roosevelt had a short, uneventful VP term, becoming President in 1901. As President, he was known for "Trust Busting," passing anti-monopoly laws, and pioneering national parks.

Re-elected once in 1904, Teddy decided not to run again in 1908 and threw his support behind William Howard Taft. When Taft did not govern the way Roosevelt thought he should, Teddy decided to start his own political party (the Progressive, or "Bull Moose" Party) in 1912 and run against his successor. While campaigning in Milwaukee, a potential assassin shot at him, hitting him in the chest. Teddy insisted upon giving his speech before being rushed to the hospital.

Teddy split the vote, handing the Democratic candidate Woodrow Wilson, with his VP Thomas Marshall, the victory. Teddy spent his retirement writing more books until he succumbed to rheumatism and an arterial blood clot in 1919. He was buried in Oyster Bay, New York.

Alan Naldrett

If the Vice-Presidency had been decided by the most awesome mustache, Fairbanks would've won easy.

CHARLES W. FAIRBANKS— MORE THAN A TOWN IN ALASKA

Charles Fairbanks (1852-1918) followed in the tradition of his fellow Hoosiers Thomas Marshall, Schuyler Colfax and Thomas Hendricks—he became Vice-President. Later VPs from Indiana were Dan Quayle and Mike Pence—making six in all from the Hoosier State.

Fairbanks was born in Unionville Center, Ohio in 1852, graduated from Ohio Wesleyan University, and moved to Indianapolis, Indiana. He worked as a railroad financier and attorney under Jay Gould. After befriending President William McKinley, he was asked to give the keynote speech at the 1896 Republican Convention. He parlayed this into a successful run for the Senate from Indiana in 1897 to 1905. He served on a committee that helped solve the Alaskan boundary question. Subsequently, the town of Fairbanks, Alaska was named for him.

He envisioned big things for himself. He made a considerable fortune representing bankrupt railroads and then serving as their Chief Officer or President. He declined the Vice-Presidency under William McKinley because he wanted to wait "for the top nod to come." When McKinley was shot, and his VP Teddy Roosevelt became President, Fairbanks realized he would've been President if he had accepted the Vice-Presidency.

He didn't make that mistake twice, taking the #2 slot on the ticket in 1904, under Teddy Roosevelt. When Teddy didn't run again, Fairbanks unsuccessfully tried for the Republican Party nomination for President in the 1908 contest, not garnering enough support in the Party. Unfortunately, the *Nation* magazine once remarked about one of his speeches, "No public speaker can more quickly drive an audience to despair."

In 1916, Fairbanks again announced his candidacy for President. He settled for the Vice-Presidential slot again with Charles Evans Hughes as the Presidential candidate. They lost to Woodrow Wilson and Thomas Marshall.

With failing health, Fairbanks returned home to Indianapolis to practice law. He died of nephritis on June 4, ~~1898~~ *1918* and was buried in Crown Hill Cemetery.

Alan Naldrett

JAMES SCHOOLCRAFT SHERMAN— HAD BEST VICE-PRESIDENTIAL MAUSOLEUM

If I had to pick a "least-known Vice-President," I think my pick would be James S. Sherman (1855-1912), although it might take me a minute or two to remember his name. Sherman was the 27th Vice-President, serving under President William Howard Taft from 1909 to 1912. He was the seventh Vice-President to die in office.

James Sherman was born in Utica, New York in 1855, went to Hamilton College, studied law, and was admitted to the New York bar in 1880. He became Mayor of Utica in 1884 at the age of 29. He was related to Roger Sherman, signer of the Declaration of Independence, and General William Tecumseh Sherman, of Civil-War fame.

Sherman was a wealthy businessman from Utica, New York, inheriting the New Hartford Canning Company, and becoming President of the Utica Trust Company.

Sherman was elected to the House of Representatives from New York in 1886 and went on to serve 20 years in the House. He participated in a filibuster wherein he chastised the Democrats with a poem comparing them to lightning bugs:

The lighting bug is brilliant,

But it hasn't any mind;

It stumbles through existence

With its headlight on behind.

Teddy Roosevelt wanted a New York candidate to balance the ticket with Taft, his self-appointed successor, he looked to Republican James "Sunny Jim" Sherman. In the election of 1908, Taft and Sherman won.

Sherman is the only VP whose bust in the Senate is wearing glasses. In fact, his work on behalf of Native Americans—he was head of the Committee on Indian Affairs for years as part of his House of Representatives work—got him an honorary "Indian name." It was *Wau-be-ka-chuck*, which reputedly means "four eyes."

WILLIAM H. TAFT   JAMES S. SHERMAN

Sherman had a scandal regarding his Chairmanship of the Committee of Indian Affairs. During the Presidential election of 1908, Sherman was accused by a California lawyer named Edmund Burke of obtaining tens of thousands of acres of Native American land in New Mexico through his influence on the Committee of Indian Affairs and bribery. The Democrats never took it any further and the Republicans claimed it was just an attempt to slander Sherman.

President Taft was an avid golfer and was happy to hear that

Sherman played too. But after seeing Sherman's poor play, he avoided future golf expeditions with him. Even though Sherman's son was a noted golfer, Sherman himself was not a sportsman. He once provided uniforms for a local baseball team, but this didn't prevent him from being voted off the team.

Sherman inherited the Harford Canning Company and therefore fought against labeling laws. This changed his nickname among many from "Sunny Jim" and "Trusty Jim" to "Short-Weight Jim." He was also chastised for employing children under 16 in his factory.

Sherman had an uneventful Vice-Presidential term and was set to be the candidate in the Election of 1912, the first Republican Vice-President up until then to be re-nominated. However, Sherman died of Bright's Disease right before the election, too late to replace him on the ticket. Taft lost to Wilson, due to Teddy Roosevelt running his own third-party candidacy and splitting the Republican vote, giving the Democrats and Woodrow Wilson a victory. The fact that Taft's running mate Sherman had died couldn't have helped either. Sherman was the seventh VP to die in office. What Sherman lacked in luster during his life, he made up for in death by having the most elaborate Vice-Presidential burying-place.

THOMAS RILEY MARSHALL— CIGAR PROMOTER

Thomas R. Marshall (1854-1925) was not the biggest fan of the office of Vice-President, but he is probably the one with the best sense of humor about it. He served as the 28th Vice-President for two terms under President Woodrow Wilson, from 1913 until 1921.

Marshall went to Wabash College and upon graduation opened a law firm in Columbia City, Indiana. For many years he built up his law firm. In 1880, he ran for prosecuting attorney from his district but lost.

In 1895 he met and married Lois Kimsey and she helped him overcome his alcoholism. He became a seasoned temperance speaker and well-known Democrat, helping fellow Democrats campaign. In 1906 he was nominated for Congress but refused, hinting he would rather be Governor.

He then received support from the party bosses to run for Governor in the 1908 election. Because of a split in the Republican Party, he barely beat his opponent James E. Watson, with 48.1% of the vote to Watson's 48%.

Marshall home in Columbia City, Indiana

Marshall met Kate Hooper and was engaged to her when she died in 1882. Her death the day before their wedding caused Marshall to find solace in a bottle and he became a functioning alcoholic.

Marshall was Indiana's first Democratic governor in 20 years. In his administration, laws were passed banning child labor and exposing public corruption. As a Progressive Democratic Governor, he came to the attention of the national Democratic Party bosses and was tapped to be Wilson's Vice-Presidential candidate in 1912. Marshall at first refused the office but reconsidered when Woodrow Wilson told him he would be given lots of duties as Vice-President.

With the Republicans splitting their votes between incumbent William Howard Taft and Teddy Roosevelt's Progressive (Bull Moose) Party, Wilson and Marshall were victorious. However, Wilson did not live up to his promise to give the Vice-President lots of duties. Marshall took up residence in the Senate and became known for his wit. His most famous quip occurred during a Senator's address on what the country needs. Marshall, presiding over the Senate, said "What this country needs is a good 5-cent cigar."

Marshall was fond of telling the story, "Once upon a time a man had two sons. One went away to sea and the other became Vice-President. Neither were ever heard from again." He also said, remarking upon the Vice-Presidency, "Just know that you mean nothing, don't make waves, and you'll get your paycheck every Friday."

Although re-elected in 1916 along with Wilson, their relationship was said to be, "functioning animosity." The election of 1916 had both major Vice-Presidential candidates from Indiana (James Sherman was from Indiana). Marshall was the first VP to win a second term since John C. Calhoun.

Marshall was not in the loop when Wilson suffered a stroke and his wife superseded the Vice-President by deciding who the President would see and what paperwork he would look at.

Upon leaving the office, he wrote his Vice-Presidential successor, Calvin Coolidge, giving him his "sincere condolences." He moved to Indianapolis and started private practice in law, while serving on a few foundations. Upon his retirement, he remarked, "I don't want to work. But I wouldn't mind being Vice-President again."

On June 1, 1925, he succumbed to a heart attack and was buried in Crown Hill Cemetery in Indianapolis.

CALVIN COOLIDGE —SILENT, SLEEPY CAL

John Calvin Coolidge (1872-1933) managed to escape President Warren G. Harding's Teapot Dome scandal. So, there was little objection when Coolidge assumed the Presidency, sworn in by his father, a judge.

Coolidge was the only President or VP born on July 4. He had a quiet childhood on the farm in Plymouth, Vermont. He went to Amherst College in 1891 and graduated with honors in 1895. He was then admitted to the Massachusetts bar in 1897. He was elected a councilman at Northampton, Massachusetts in 1899 and went on to be city solicitor, clerk of the courts, a member of the Massachusetts state legislature, mayor of Northampton, a state senator, Lieutenant Governor, and then Governor of Massachusetts.

REPUBLICAN STANDARD BEARERS
1924

— TWO GREAT AMERICANS —

Coolidge gained national fame for his level-headed handling of the Boston Police Strike in 1919. This was apparently enough for the Massachusetts delegation to promote him for President at the 1920 Republican Convention. When the convention nominated Harding for President, they next nominated Coolidge for Vice-President. The Harding-Coolidge team beat the Democratic team of James Cox and Franklin D. Roosevelt by an electoral vote of 404-212.

Coolidge was the first Vice-President to be admitted to Cabinet meetings and took an active part in President Harding's government. After Harding's mysterious death in the Palace Hotel in San Francisco, Coolidge dealt with the fallout from the Teapot Dome scandal and otherwise was not known as a very robust President. sleeping 11 hours at night and taking an afternoon nap of a few hours during the day. He was also known for his reticence and was called "Silent Cal."

An often-repeated story was the one where a woman was seated next to Calvin Coolidge and told him, "I've made a bet that I can get you to say more than two words!" To which Coolidge famously replied, "You lose."

Coolidge successfully ran for a Presidential term in his own right in 1924, with Charles Dawes as his running-mate. When his term was over, Coolidge declined running for another one and retired to Northampton, Massachusetts. He wrote newspaper columns and books until he died of a heart attack in 1933 and was buried in Plymouth, Vermont.

Alan Naldrett

CHARLES DAWES--IT'S ALL IN THE NOBEL GAME

Charles Gates Dawes (1865-1951) was perhaps the most accomplished Vice-President no one ever remembers. From winning a Nobel Prize to writing a hit song, he was a man of many talents.

Dawes was born in Marietta, Ohio, the son of Rufus Republic Dawes, who was a Civil War General, a lumber merchant, and a member of the House of Representatives from 1881 to 1883. His great-great grandfather was William Dawes, who also made the same ride as Paul Revere, warning that the British were coming.

Charles went to Marietta Academy, and Marietta College, where he got a bachelor's degree in Civil Engineering in 1884. He minored in music and studied piano and flute. He earned a law degree at the Cincinnati Law School at the age of 19 in 1886. He got a job with the Marietta, Columbus and Northern Ohio Railway Company as a civil engineer and went on to be the chief engineer for construction.

In 1887 he moved to Lincoln, Nebraska and joined his cousin's law firm, Dawes, Coffroth, and Cunningham. Their law firm was in the same building, two floors up, as future Presidential candidate William Jennings Bryan. Besides his law practice, Dawes became the Vice-President of Lincoln Packing Company, gaining that valuable Vice-President experience.

Dawes law knowledge led him to successes in administrative re-organization of failing companies. He relocated to the Chicago area in 1895. He eventually developed a business empire, starting with the North Shore Gas Company in 1900, and ultimately assembling a utility holding company called Metropolitan Gas and Electric Company, which owned seven companies, with 28 plants, in 10 different states.

In 1896, Dawes became active in Republican politics, and headed William McKinley's Presidential campaign in Illinois. As a reward, McKinley appointed Dawes the Comptroller of the Currency, a position Dawes held from 1898 to 1901. In 1901, Dawes wished to move on to the U.S. Senate and figured he would get an appointment due to his McKinley connections. Unfortunately, McKinley's 1901 assassination ended that idea, as Teddy Roosevelt, the new President, did not have the same sympathies. After the Senate rebuff, Dawes returned to manage his businesses, including heading the Dawes bank.

In 1911, he composted "Melody in A Major," and played it for a violinist friend who had it published. The sheet music was a big seller, and was revived a few times after its initial popularity, most notably in the 1920s and 1930s as a favorite of master violinist Fritz Kreisler, and in the 1940s by popular big band leader Tommy Dorsey. The tune has often been referred to as "Dawes Melody."

The song went on to further fame as Carl Sigman put lyrics to the melody. Under the title, "It's All in the Game," the song went on to ac-claim as a #1 single by Tommy Edwards in 1951, was subsequently re-corded by multiple artists, and is now considered a classic.

In World War I, Dawes became a Brigadier General under General Pershing, whom he knew from his Nebraska law days, and oversaw pur-chasing for the military. He testified before a Congressional Committee about military spending and at one point used the phrase that he would become known for, "Hell and Maria," which he used as an exclamation in his statement. The phrase was, "Hell and Maria! We weren't trying to keep a set of books, we were trying to win the war!"

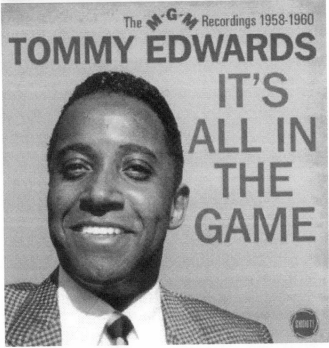

Dawes served as Director of Bureau of the Budget in 1921, and in 1923, as Chairman of the Allied Reparations Commission, he put together the "Dawes Plan," which provided debt release for post-war Germany. When the plan was adopted in 1924, Charles Dawes was awarded the 1925 Nobel Peace Prize.

When Governor Frank Lowden of Illinois turned down the Vice-Presidency at the 1924 Republican Convention, the party went to their second choice, Charles Dawes. Dawes, who had only a failed Senate candidacy to his credit in running for office, accepted the VP bid. Calvin Coolidge was the Republican Presidential candidate, and incumbent, having taken over the office upon the death of Warren G. Harding.

The ticket of Coolidge and Dawes were up against Democratic opponents John W. Davis and his VP Charles W. Bryan, the brother of William Jennings Bryan and former Nebraska Governor. Dawes and Coolidge defeated the pair, 382 electoral votes to 136, making Dawes the 30th Vice-President.

CALVIN COOLIDGE   CHARLES G. DAWES
FOR PRESIDENT   FOR VICE-PRESIDENT

Dawe's Vice-Presidency had an inauspicious beginning, as a speech he gave chastising Congress for their filibuster rules received more attention than Coolidge's inaugural speech. Coolidge was also not happy when Dawes was sleeping in a nearby hotel, waiting to go to the Senate chambers to cast a tie-breaking vote if needed. But Dawes failed to wake up and missed one vote, causing the Republicans to miss getting the bill passed.

While Vice-President, Dawes supported farm relief programs, naval appropriations, and bank reform.

When President Coolidge announced his retirement in 1928, Dawes followed suit. He was the next ambassador to Great Britain, from 1929 to 1932. After serving briefly as the director of the Reconstruction Finance Corporation (RFC), he quit to resume his concentration on his banking businesses.

Dawes was a philanthropist, helping to fund the Chicago Symphony Orchestra, and forming the Mary Dawes Hotel for Women and the Rufus Fearing Dawes Hotel for Destitute Men, providing housing for impoverished men and women.

Dawes died at him home in Evanston, Illinois at the age of 85. Ironically, the year he died, 1951, was the same year his composition "It's All in the Game" became the #1 Song of the Year. He was buried in Chicago's Rosehill Cemetery, and upon his death of coronary thrombosis, had been married to his wife Caro for 62 years.

CHARLES CURTIS— BEST NATIVE AMERICAN VICE-PRESIDENT EVER

Charles Curtis (1860-1936) was the first—and to date the only—Native American Vice-President. This is how he is referred, although he was only one-eighth Native American, on his mother's side. This isn't even enough to earn casino money! He was partly raised on the Kaw Indian Reservation in Kansas and learned to hunt and ride horses bareback there. He attended public schools in Topeka and used his horse-riding skills to become a jockey at a young age.

VP Charles Curtis filling in for Coolidge by tossing out the first baseball of the season.

Curtis studied law with local attorneys and politicians he met while driving a cab. He was awarded membership in the Kansas bar in 1881. This led him to be elected to the position of prosecuting attorney of Shawnee County. In 1886, he was elected to the U.S. House of Representatives and in 1907 was elected to the U.S. Senate. He was re-elected and stayed in his Senate seat until 1929, serving as Senate whip from 1915 to 1924, when he became the majority leader for the Republicans.

In 1928, when Coolidge decided not to run for another term, Curtis declared his candidacy. He didn't get the Presidential nod, but he was selected to be number two on the ticket under former Commerce Secretary Herbert Hoover. Hoover and Curtis campaigned widely and beat their Democratic opponents, Governor Al Smith of New York and their VP nominee Joseph T. Robinson of Arkansas, 444 to 87 electoral votes.

Curtis did well as Vice-President, casting 3 tie-breaking votes as President of the Senate. He was considered the wise old political veteran, offsetting Hoover, who had never held an elective office. Unfortuneatly, the stock market crash and the Great Depression happened on Hoover's watch and the ticket was soundly defeated by the Democratic ticket of Franklin Roosevelt of New York and John Nance Garner of Texas in 1932.

Curtis was 69 years old when he began his VP term, and 73 when he finished. He returned to his law practice for three years before he died in 1936 at the age of 76 and was buried in Topeka, Kansas.

JOHN NANCE GARNER—A BUCKET OF WARM "SPIT"

John Nance Garner (1868-1967) was famous for calling the office of Vice-President "not worth a bucket of warm spit." Except he probably used a different word that rhymes with "spit."

Garner was born in a log cabin near a village named Detroit in Red River County, Texas. Although his early schooling was spotty, he spent a year at Vanderbilt University and studied law with a lawyer in Clarksville, Texas. He was admitted to the Texas bar in 1890 and opened his own law office. Moving to Uvalde, Garner became adept at investing in land, cattle, banks, and other businesses.

In 1898, Garner ran for and won a seat in the Texas legislature, to which he was re-elected to. While there, he supported making the cactus the Texas State Flower (the Bluebonnet won). Because of this, his nickname became "Cactus Jack." In 1902 he was elected to the U.S. House of Representatives, where he served until elected Vice-President. He was the Speaker of the House from 1931 to 1933.

When Garner was a Presidential candidate in 1932, he realized he wouldn't have enough votes to win, so he threw his support behind Franklin D. Roosevelt and gave him his delegates. In appreciation, Roosevelt made Garner his Vice-President. When FDR ran for a second term, Garner stayed on the ticket and served two terms as VP. His term encompassed the Great Depression.

In 1940, when FDR was renominated again for a third term, Garner informed him that he wished to retire. Garner moved home to Uvalde and was the longest-lived VP, dying just 15 days short of his 99th birthday.

Alan Naldrett

HENRY A. WALLACE —FIRST SOCIALIST VICE-PRESIDENT

When John Nance Garner wanted to retire after two terms as Veep, FDR needed a man for his third term, so he went to his Cabinet and drafted his Secretary of Agriculture, Henry A. Wallace (1888-1965). Wallace was a farmer and a son of a farmer. His father served as the Secretary of Agriculture under Presidents Harding and Coolidge.

Wallace was born in Adair County, Iowa and grew up doing farm work. He went to the Iowa State College and studied scientific farming, graduating in 1910. He developed a very good hybrid corn and edited the family newspaper, *Wallace's Farmer*, which was started by his grandfather.

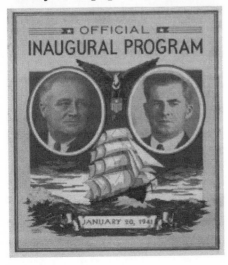

Wallace began to develop an interest in the political side of agriculture in 1920 and started lobbying for farmers' interests in Washington, D.C. He was noticed by Franklin Roosevelt, who was Governor of New York at the time. When FDR became President, he asked Wallace to be his Secretary of Agriculture. While Secretary, Wallace worked on soil conservation and controlled agricultural production issues.

Wallace continued as Secretary of Agriculture for both of FDR's first two terms. When FDR needed another Vice-President to replace his previous VP, John Garner, who didn't care to run again, he asked Wallace. Wallace was popular with the farmers, minority groups, and working people. Wallace accepted and served a term as Vice-President.

As VP, Wallace was chairman of the Economic Defense Board and championed liberal causes. Roosevelt used him to fill in for him for various functions and included him in Cabinet meetings. When the Democrats thought he was TOO liberal, they refused to approve him for FDR's fourth term, choosing Harry Truman instead. FDR then appointed Wallace as his Secretary of Commerce.

Upon FDR's death in 1945, he was succeeded by his new Vice-President Harry Truman. Wallace remained as Truman's Secretary of Commerce until 1946, when Wallace started to disagree with many of Truman's policies.

In 1948, Wallace started his own political party, the Progressive Party. "Progressive" has been a popular name for U.S. political parties. There was Teddy Roosevelt's "Bull Moose" Progressive Party of 1912, and the Progressive Party of Wisconsin's Robert La Follette of 1924, not to mention the Progressive Parties of Minnesota and California.

Henry Wallace's Progressive Party of 1948 served primarily as a vehicle for the Presidential run of candidate Henry Wallace. The party platform called for desegregation, national health care, nationalization of the energy industries, and other progressive concepts. The party was derided for being Socialistic and Communistic and only received 2.4% of the vote. The Dixiecrats' candidate Strom Thurmond was also in the race and earned 39 electoral votes, with about 3.1% of the vote.

After the election Wallace returned to farming and agricultural research. He died in 1965 in Danbury, Connecticut at the age of 77.

HARRY S TRUMAN— ITCHY TRIGGER FINGER

Harry Truman (1884-1972) had several occupations before becoming Vice-President, and then President, upon the death of Franklin Roosevelt. Although he was famous for owning a haberdashery business, he also was the timekeeper on a railroad construction crew, a bank clerk, a mailroom assistant at a newspaper, and a bookkeeper. He then moved back to Independence, Missouri, to take over the family farm. During World War I, Truman joined the Army as a Lieutenant and was attached to an artillery unit.

When Truman was young, the family was too poor for him to go to college. But Truman went into politics anyway, studying at the Kansas City Law School from 1923 to 1925. He then went into politics, first as a county judge of Jackson County, Missouri, then as the presiding judge from 1926 until 1934. In 1934, he is elected to the U.S. Senate from Kansas.

Harry Truman birthplace

As Senator, he became Chairman of the Special Senate Committee to investigate the National Defense Program for corruption and waste. This brought him national recognition, and when FDR was looking for a Vice-President to replace Henry Wallace, Truman was chosen by the Democratic Convention.

After winning the election, just 83 days later Roosevelt succumbed to polio and Truman was sworn in as President. These were the final days of World War II and Truman made the decision to use the first Atomic Bomb on the Japanese to end the war sooner. A bomb was dropped on Hiroshima, and a few days later, on Nagasaki, Japan.

The Japanese sued for peace and World War II ended. With the end of the war, the Truman Doctrine and Marshal Plan were implemented to aid in recovery. The United Nations was formed.

In 1948 Truman ran for re-election and won, against all odds. His Vice-President Alben Barkley and Truman defeated Thomas Dewey of New York and future Chief Justice of the Supreme Court Earl Warren.

Truman declined to run in 1948 and retired to Independence, Missouri, where he wrote his memoirs. He died in 1972 after a long illness and was buried in Independence.

A LBEN BARKLEY —THE VICE-PRESIDENT'S VICE-PRESIDENT

Alben Barkley (1877-1956) was born in a log cabin in Graves County, Kentucky. He grew up on a tobacco farm and then went to Marvin College in Clinton, Kentucky, graduating in 1897. He continued his education, studying law at Emory College in Georgia and the University of Virginia Law School. He joined the Kentucky bar and opened a law practice.

In 1905 Barkley became prosecuting attorney of McCracken County until 1909, and then became judge of the county court. In 1912, he ran for and won a seat in the U.S. House of Representatives, representing Kentucky.

Barkley was in favor of Prohibition and was against pari-mutuel betting. Although he lost his bid for Kentucky governor in 1926, he won a U.S. Senate seat in 1927. He had a distinguished career as Senator, serving through World War II and helping the legislative branch concentrate on the domestic front, while the executive branch was concentrated on foreign affairs.

When Barkley gave an energizing speech in favor of Truman during the 1948 Democratic Convention, Truman selected him for his Vice-President. The election was close and contentious, with Truman behind the whole way, but the Truman-Barkley ticket was declared the winner the day after the election.

With Truman preoccupied during the Korean War, Barkley was very active filling in for Truman during the 1948-1952 Presidential term. When Truman decided not to seek another term, Barkley considered running, but was informed by Labor representatives that no one would support him due to his age—Barkley was the oldest serving Vice-President. Upon withdrawing from the nomination, he received a 45-minute ovation at the Democratic Convention.

Barkley was a well-loved VP, and was affectionately given the nickname, the "Veep." Truman had the Vice-Presidential Seal and Flag designed for him. Although a few eyebrows were raised when he became the first (and to-date-only) Vice-President to get married while in office. He married Jane Hadley, who was 38. Barkley was 71 and Hadley was 38, a 33-year age difference.

In 1954, after his VP term, Barkley was re-elected to the Senate. He was still a Senator when he died in 1956.

R ICHARD NIXON— CHECKERS NOT CHESS

The Saga of Richard Nixon (1913-1994) includes a Vice-Presidential story like no other. Although he is well-known as a President, who both opened China to the U.S., and resigned due to the Watergate scandal, he would have had renown as a memorable Vice-President. He would be known for both the Kitchen Debate, where he debated Russian Premier Nikita Khrushchev on the merits of Communism vs. Capitalism, and the infamous "Checkers Speech," where Nixon went on TV to defend his use of campaign money by referring to his daughters' pet cocker spaniel Checkers.

Nixon was born in Yorba Linda, California to a Quaker family. The family moved to Whittier, California, and Nixon went on to Whittier College where he played football for the Whittier Poets, was on the debate team, and was a campus leader. He went to Duke Law School on a scholarship and passed the California bar in 1937. He returned to Whittier and opened a law office, which he operated until 1942.

Checkers and Nixon

In 1942 he worked briefly for the Office for Emergency Management in Washington, D.C. and then was commissioned a lieutenant in the U.S. Navy. Serving during World War II, Nixon mustered out in 1946 and ran for the House of Representatives in California. Winning after a series of debates with the incumbent, he was re-elected in 1948 while premiering many of the "red-baiting" tactics of the day. In 1950 he employed the same tactics to win a Senate seat and in two years parlayed that into a Vice-Presidential nomination.

In 1952 General Dwight D. Eisenhower, with his running mate Richard M. Nixon, beat Democratic Party candidates Adlai Stevenson and his VP John Parkman.

Nixon presided over Security Council and Cabinet meetings in Eisenhower's absence and was given other new duties as Vice-President. In 1956 the ticket was re-elected, in a repeat of the previous election with Stevenson as the candidate. Stevenson's change of VP running mate to Estes Kefauver didn't change his luck, however, as Ike Eisenhower and Dick Nixon won again.

When Ike retired in 1960, Nixon announced his candidacy. He secured the nomination for President from the Republican Party, with Henry Cabot Lodge for his running mate. He successfully debated his opponent John F. Kennedy, but narrowly lost the election, even though there were strong hints of Democratic corruption.

When Nixon lost his quest to be Governor of California in 1962, he famously, and prematurely, said to the Press, "You don't have Nixon to kick around anymore, because, gentlemen, this is my last press conference."

After private law practice from 1963 until 1967 New York, in 1968 he made his comeback. He announced his candidacy for President and won the nomination. At the convention, he introduced his Vice-Presidential pick, Spiro Agnew. The Nixon and Agnew team went on to beat the Democratic team of Hubert Humphrey and Edmund Muskie.

Nixon and Agnew went on to soundly beat Democrats George McGovern and Sargent Shriver in the 1972 election, but by the time the term was over both principals had resigned. Richard Nixon was brought down by the Watergate scandal which involved bugging the Democratic Party's offices and Nixon having tapes that he made himself that incriminated him.

After resigning the Presidency in 1974, Nixon was pardoned by his successor Gerald Ford. He spent his remaining years writing books and consulting.

Alan Naldrett

LYNDON JOHNSON —REMEMBER CIVIL RIGHTS, NOT VIETNAM

The early days of Lyndon Johnson (1908-1973) were spent on a Texas farm. He went to school in Johnson City, Texas where he was president of his senior class. He worked on a road crew as a laborer to raise money for college. He attended Southwest Texas Teacher's College in 1927 where he was editor of the school newspaper.

He graduated in 1930 and started teaching debating and public speaking at Sam Houston High School. In 1931 he began working for Congressman Richard Kleberg. In 1935, FDR appointed Johnson to be the head of the National Youth Administration in Texas.

In 1937, Lyndon ran for and won a special election to fill a vacancy in the House, caused by the death of Representative James P. Buchanan. Johnson parlayed the new position to win election to the Senate in 1948, becoming the Senate Whip in 1951.

In 1960, Johnson announced his candidacy for President but lost the nomination to John Kennedy. Instead, he accepted the Vice-Presidential nomination. Kennedy and Johnson went on to win a close race against their Republican opponents, Richard Nixon and Henry Cabot Lodge.

As VP, Johnson kept busy filling in for Kennedy at events, attending Cabinet meetings, and throwing his considerable influence around Congress, rallying support for the Democratic platform, including civil rights reform—an issue he would be successful at.

On a campaign stop in Dallas, Johnson was present when Kennedy was assassinated, making Johnson President. As President he was successful at passing civil rights legislation and launching a "War on Poverty." In the wake of Kennedy's assassination and the nation's fear of Goldwater, Johnson and his running mate Hubert Humphrey beat the Republican ticket of Barry Goldwater and William Miller by a landslide in 1964.

LBJ birthplace

By the end of his first term, Johnson announced he wouldn't seek another, because of his unpopularity due to the U.S. escalation of the War in Vietnam.

Johnson retired to his ranch in Stonewall, Texas and died in 1973. He was buried on the Johnson Ranch.

HUBERT H. HUMPHREY —DUMP THE HUMP?

Hubert Horatio Humphrey (1911-1978) was the Vice-President of Lyndon Johnson and the Democratic candidate for President in 1968.

Humphrey was born in Wallace, South Dakota, the son of a pharmacist who owned a drug store. Humphrey worked in the store when he was young and went to the University of Minnesota and then the Denver College of Pharmacy to earn a degree in pharmacy. After practicing pharmacy for a few years, in 1937 he returned to the University of Minnesota and graduated in 1939 with a degree in political science.

After graduating with a bachelor's degree in Political Science in 1939, he achieved a master's degree in Political Science at the University of Louisiana and taught there and at the University of Minnesota. In 1943 and 1944 he taught at Macalester College in St. Paul, Minnesota.

In 1943, Humphrey ran for mayor of Minneapolis and was defeated. He tried again in 1945 and was successful. He went on to serve two terms as mayor. He instituted reforms and started programs for the poor.

In 1949, he was elected to his first term as Senator from Minnesota. Re-elected in 1954 and 1960, he became the Senate Majority Whip in 1961. He was widely known to support liberal programs and was instrumental in getting Johnson's Civil Rights bill passed in 1964.

When Johnson decided to run for President in 1964, he chose Humphrey as his running-mate. After the Johnson-Humphrey team's landslide victory, Humphrey went on to declare his own candidacy for President in 1968 when Johnson declared he would not run again.

Since Johnson's popularity was low due to the War in Vietnam, Humphrey and his running mate Edmund Muskie suffered through and lost a close election to Republican Richard Nixon and his running mate, Spiro Agnew.

After the election, Humphrey returned to teaching at his two previous places of employment. In 1970, he ran for the Senate and won. Despite a diagnosis of bladder cancer, Humphrey won re-election in 1976 but succumbed to the disease in 1978 before he could finish his term. He was buried in Minneapolis.

S PIRO T. AGNEW— NATTERING NEGATIVE NABOBS OF MALFEASANCE

Spiro "Ted" Agnew (1918-1996) was only the second Vice-President to resign, although the first VP to resign, Calhoun, had more honorable reasons. Agnew pleaded nolo contendre to tax evasion, a lower charge than his original indictment for bribery while Governor of Maryland.

Agnew was born in Baltimore, Maryland to a father who owned a Greek restaurant. His father changed the family name from Anagnostopoulos to Agnew.

Agnew went to college at Johns Hopkins University and then transferred to Baltimore Law School. He worked days and went to classes at night. He received his law degree in 1947 and moved to Towson, Maryland. There he got a job with a law firm, before starting his own practice. He switched from the Democratic Party to the Republican Party and started helping with election campaigns.

In 1957 he was appointed to the Baltimore County Zoning Board of Appeals and was named County Executive in 1962. He held this position until 1966 when he ran for and won the race for Governor of Maryland.

At the 1968 Republican Convention, Agnew put candidate Richard Nixon's name in for the Republican Presidential nomination. Once Nixon had the nomination he announced Agnew as his choice for Vice-President.

The Nixon-Agnew team barely beat the Humphrey-Muskie team of the Democrats. During Nixon's first term, Agnew made many speeches on behalf of the Nixon Administration.

After victory in the 1972 election over the Democratic team of George McGovern and Sargent Shriver, things started to unravel for the team. Besides Nixon's Watergate problems, Agnew had some of his own. Baltimore's U.S. Attorney George Beall uncovered evidence that Agnew had accepted bribes and kickback money from real estate developers in return for lucrative building contracts.

Because of his own possible impeachment, Nixon did not provide any White House support for Agnew. In August of 1973, when the press found out about the story, Agnew at first called the allegations "damned lies" and announced that he had the President's support in fighting the charges. But Nixon's new Chief of Staff, Alexander Haig, asked Agnew to resign because Beall had an airtight case. Agnew at first refused, but by September the plea bargaining had begun. Agnew insisted that the statute that prevented the President from being prosecuted for a crime while in office also applied to the Vice-President. The Justice Department ruled that the rule applied only to the sitting President.

As Agnew fought his battles, public opinion was turning against him. Finally, on October 10, 1973, Agnew pleaded no contest to income tax evasion, receiving a $10,000 fine and 3-year suspended jail sentence. He gave Secretary of State Henry Kissinger his written resignation as VP later that afternoon.

Five days after Agnew's resignation he gave a "farewell address" where he continued to proclaim his innocence and blame all his problems on the media. He maintained his innocence for two decades. But still his bust was not added to the Vice-President's section of Statuary Hall until 1995, when Agnew was 76. He died a year later in 1996.

GERALD FORD—THE FIRST NON-ELECTED VICE-PRESIDENT (AND PRESIDENT)

Gerald "Jerry" Ford (1913-2006) was the first unelected Vice-President and President. A long-time Congressman from Grand Rapids, Michigan, he burst out of semi-obscurity to become Vice-President. Ford was the first VP selected under the new 25th Amendment, which laid out new rules for appointing a new Vice-President when the reigning VP resigns, dies, or becomes incapacitated. When Nixon's VP Spiro Agnew resigned after a kickback scandal, Nixon appointed Representative Gerald Ford to replace him and Ford was quickly approved by Congress.

Gerald Ford was born as Leslie King but took the name of his adopted father and ditched the "Leslie," becoming Gerald Ford, Jr. He was born in Omaha, Nebraska and upon remarriage moved to Grand Rapids, Michigan with his mother and Gerald, Sr.

Putting himself through college by waiting tables and washing dishes, Ford attended the University of Michigan, playing on the football team and named Most Valuable Player in 1934. After attaining his bachelor's degree from Michigan, he attended and graduated from Yale Law School, setting up practice in Grand Rapids. He served in the U.S. Navy during World War II, and in 1945 returned to his law practice, marrying Elizabeth ("Betty") Bloomer and having four children.

In 1949 Ford was elected to the U.S. House of Representative for the Grand Rapids area and served with distinction for 25 years. In 1965 he was named the House Minority Leader. He was then chosen to be Vice-President and served as the 40th VP from December 1973 until Nixon's resignation in August 1974.

Ford served out the rest of Nixon's Presidential term and under the 25th Amendment, appointed Nelson Rockefeller as his Vice-President. In 1976, he became the Republican nominee for President, after besting future President Ronald Reagan at the Convention. With his running mate Bob Dole, Ford lost to the Democratic team of Jimmy Carter and his VP Walter Mondale, in a close race that saw Ford win more states, but Carter win more electoral votes.

Ford remained active in the Republican Party until his death in 2006 at 93 years old. He was buried at the Ford Museum in Grand Rapids.

N ELSON ROCKEFELLER— DONATED THE VEEP MANSION

Nelson "Rocky" Rockefeller (1908-1979) was the second Vice-President appointed under the provisions of the 25th Amendment. He was born in Bar Harbor, Maine into the richest family in America. Rocky's grandfather was John D. Rockefeller, who made a fortune in oil and was the nation's first billionaire.

Rocky went to Dartmouth College and graduated in 1930 with a degree in economics. In 1958, he successfully ran for Governor of New York after holding positions in government under Presidents Roosevelt, Truman, and Eisenhower. He was re-elected three times as New York Governor, longer than any other. He unsuccessfully sought the Presidential nomination in 1964 and 1968.

Unlike most of the people in this book, Nelson Rockefeller was known more for his last name than for being Vice-President. As one of a family of billionaires, he not only donated the Naval Observatory Mansion in 1977 that has become the Vice-Presidential Mansion, but he also spent his own money to have the Vice-Presidential seal redesigned.

Nelson Rockefeller died of a heart attack and was cremated and buried in the private family plot.

Ice-skating at Rockefeller Center in 2017.

WALTER MONDALE —FIRST DEBATING VEEP

Walter "Fritz" Mondale (1928-) was born to a Ceylon, Minnesota farmer and minister. Following in the footsteps of another Minnesota VP, Hubert Humphrey, he went to Macalester College and then transferred to the University of Minnesota, graduating in 1951. After spending two years in the Army during the Korean War, he entered the University of Minnesota Law School and graduated in 1956. Practicing law for several years, he married Joan Adams and had three children.

Mondale got appointed to be the Minnesota Attorney General in 1960 to fill a vacancy. He then ran for and won another term. While he was still a Representative, he was appointed to fill the Senate seat vacated by Hubert Humphrey when he became Vice-President. He was elected to the Senate on his own in 1966 and 1972 and became known for being a spokesperson for consumer and minority interests.

Mondale and Humphrey

Mondale's running mate, Geraldine Ferraro

Mondale left the Senate to run as VP with Jimmy Carter. Together they defeated President Gerald Ford and Bob Dole. Mondale and Dole (later a losing candidate) were the first Vice-Presidents to have a debate.

Mondale served honorably as the 42nd Vice-President and campaigned for the 1980 election while Carter ran the country. Mondale returned to his Minnesota law practice when he and Carter were defeated in their re-election bid by Ronald Reagan and his Vice-President, George H.W. Bush.

Mondale was selected as the Democratic Presidential candidate for the 1984 Presidential election, with the first female Vice-Presidential running mate, Geraldine Ferraro. His platforms included the Equal Rights Amendment, a reduction in the national debt, and a nuclear freeze. Although Mondale again lost to Ronald Reagan, Mondale went on to become an elder statesman for the Democratic Party.

From 1993 to 1996 Mondale was the U.S. Ambassador to Japan. In 2002 he narrowly lost a Senate race for his old seat. Bringing the Humphrey connection full-circle, Mondale then taught at the University of Minnesota's Hubert H. Humphrey School of Public Affairs.

Ceylon, MN in the 1920's

Alan Naldrett

GEORGE H.W. BUSH —THE PETER PRINCIPLE IN PRACTICE

George Herbert Walker Bush (1924-) was a political jack-of-all-trades. He was an U.S. Navy pilot in World War II, and then a Congressman, U.N. Ambassador, Ambassador to China, Director of the C.I.A., Vice-President, and then President.

Bush was born in Milton, Massachusetts to Dorothy and Prescott Bush. Prescott would become a Senator for Connecticut. George Bush went to Phillips Academy Prep School in Andover, Massachusetts when he was 12. When World War II came he saw active service as a pilot. Upon the end of the war he married Barbara Pierce. In 1945 he entered Yale University and graduated in 1948 with a degree in economics.

Moving to Odessa, Texas, Bush was involved in the sale of oil drill-ing bits and derricks. In 1950 he moved to Midland, Texas and started his own oil development company. While in Midland Bush became active in the Republican Party, campaigning for Ike Eisenhower in 1952 and 1956.

In 1966, Bush ran for and won a seat in the U.S. House of Representatives from Texas. He stayed in the house until 1971, when President Nixon appointed him to be the U.S. Ambassador to the United Nations. He was Chairman of the Republican National Committee in 1973 and early 1974. In 1974 President Ford appointed him as Ambassador to China. In 1976, Bush was named to be the Director of the Central Intelligence Agency (CIA).

When Bush decided to run in a few state primaries in the 1980 Presidential Race, Ronald Reagan saw he was popular with voters. At the Republican Convention that summer Reagan asked Bush to be the VP nominee on his ticket and Bush accepted. The Reagan-Bush team went on to beat the incumbent team of President Carter and VP Walter Mondale. In 1984 the same team beat Democrats Walter Mondale and Geraldine Ferraro.

Although tinged with scandal due to the Iran-Contra Affair from President Reagan's administration, Bush was nominated and won the Republican nomination for President in 1988. Bush chose Indiana Senator

Dan Quayle as his running mate. The team beat the Democratic opponents of Michael Dukakis and his VP running mate, Lloyd Bentsen.

Michael Dukakis in tank.

Bush passed a Cable TV de-regulation bill and little else during his term. His four years were most notable for the Desert Storm maneuver, where Bush organized global support to expel Saddam Hussein from Kuwait. Hussein had invaded Kuwait because he declared it to be a lost province of Iraq.

Despite the successful military action, Bush lost his re-election bid to the Democratic team of Bill Clinton and his Vice-President, Al Gore.

In retirement Bush built a home near Houston and with his wife Barbara remained active in Republican affairs, making many personal appearances. He supervised the building of his Presidential library at Texas A&M University in College Station, Texas, where his gravesite is located.

Alan Naldrett

D AN QUAYLE—YOU SAY POTATO, I SAY POTATOE

J. Danforth Quayle (1947) was the 44th Vice-President and was the VP for George H.W. Bush's only Presidential term. Although a one-term Vice-President, Quayle is probably one of the most memorable, although some would say it was in the wrong way.

Quayle never got into any political scandals. He only had one main peccadillo—making verbal gaffes. Quotes like "I love California, I practically grew up in Phoenix" abounded during Quayle's Vice-Presidential term.

Quayle was born in Indianapolis, Indiana, and moved to Paradise Valley, a suburb of Phoenix, Arizona, spending a lot of his childhood there. His maternal grandfather was Eugene C. Pulliam, who owned and founded Central Newspapers, Inc., which owned over a dozen major newspapers and was headquartered in Phoenix.

Quayle returned to Indiana, married Marilyn Tucker, and went to the Indiana University Robert H. McKinney School of Law, graduating in 1974. He opened a law practice in Huntington, Indiana and started working in the Indiana Attorney General's office in the Consumer Protection Agency. He worked as an administrative assistant to Governor Edgar Whitcomb of Indiana. Quayle was also an associate publisher of the Huntington Herald-Press. He was elected to the U.S. House of Representatives in 1976. In 1980, Quayle was elected to the Senate.

George H.W. Bush chose Quayle as his Vice-Presidential running mate in 1988 and the team went on to beat Michael Dukakis and his VP Lloyd Bentsen. During his Vice-Presidency, Quayle made official visits to 47 foreign countries and was Chairman of the American Space Council.

Quayle stayed on the ticket in 1992, when George H.W. Bush ran for re-election. It was a tight race, but the Democratic ticket of Bill Clinton and his VP Al Gore claimed victory. Third-party candidate Ross Perot took about 20% of the votes but carried no states.

After the election, Quayle joined Cerberus Capital Management in 1999, as Chairman of Global Investments. In 2000 he made a run for the Presidency but shut down his campaign early when it was evident he wasn't gaining any momentum.

The most famous Quayle anecdote occurred during his visit to a Trenton, New Jersey spelling bee. Quayle "corrected" a student's spelling of potato that was on the blackboard, by adding an "e" at the end, misspelling it "potatoe."

Quayle also was known for chastising TV character Murphy Brown for being an unmarried mother. Some of his quotes include:

- The future will be better tomorrow.
- It's time for the human race to enter the solar system.
- Unfortunately, the people of Louisiana are not racists.
- The global importance of the Middle East is that it keeps the Far East and the Near East from encroaching on each other.
- One word sums up probably the responsibility of any vice-president, and that one word is 'to be prepared'.
- If we don't succeed we run the risk of failure.
- Republicans understand the importance of bondage between a mother and child.
- Republicans have been accused of abandoning the poor. It's the other way around. They never vote for us.
- My friends, no matter how rough the road may be, we can, and we will, never, never surrender to what is right.
- People that are really very weird can get into sensitive positions and have a tremendous impact on history.
- I deserve respect for the things I did not do.
- Quite frankly, teachers are the only profession that teach our children.
- It isn't pollution that's harming the environment. It's the im-

purities in our air and water that are doing it.

- We are ready for any unforeseen event that may or may not occur.
- I have made good judgments in the past. I have made good judgments in the future.
- Space is almost infinite. As a matter of fact, we think it is infinite.
- For NASA, space is still a high priority.
- This President is going to lead us out of this recovery.
- Bank failures are caused by depositors who don't deposit enough money to cover losses due to mismanagement.
- We have a firm commitment to NATO, we are a part of NATO. We have a firm commitment to Europe. We are a part of Europe.
- I stand by all the misstatements that I've made.
- The loss of life will be irreplaceable.
- I don't watch it, but I know enough to comment on it.
- It's a very good historical book about history.

In Quayle's longtime residence of Huntington, Indiana, the Vice-Presidential Hall of Fame is. It was originally a museum that was dedicated to just Dan Quayle but expanded into a museum about all the Vice-Presidents. Included is Quayle's law degree, half-chewed up by Quayle's dog.

AL GORE—NOBEL CONSOLATION PRIZE

Albert Arnold Gore, Jr. (1948-) was the 45th Vice-President, under Bill Clinton. The team beat sitting President George H.W. Bush and his VP Dan Quayle. Al Gore was also the loser in the highly-contested U.S. 2000 Presidential Election. He is known for winning a Nobel Prize for his campaign against global warming and environmental concerns, and his subsequent film, *An Inconvenient Truth.* He is also known for saying that he invented the Internet.

Al Gore was born in Washington, D.C., the son of Albert Gore, Sr., who was a Senator from Tennessee from 1953 until 1971. When Gore was born, his father was in the House of Representatives, where he served seven terms before becoming a Senator. Gore's mother Pauline was one of the first women to earn a law degree from Vanderbilt University.

Although Gore's parents were wealthy, they were frugal, giving young Al hand-me-down clothes to wear to school. The family mostly lived in a Washington, D.C. hotel during the year and young Al spent his summers and vacations working on the family farm near Carthage, Tennessee.

Gore graduated from Harvard University in 1969 with a degree in Government. He joined the U.S. Army and was a military journalist. In 1970 he married his wife Tipper. From 1971 to 1976 he worked for the *Tennessean,* a Nashville newspaper. He concentrated on local politics and investigative pieces.

In 1976, Gore ran for and won his father's old House seat and easily won re-election in 1978, 1980, and 1982. When he led the campaign to have House proceedings televised, he gave the first speech on C-Span. In 1984, Gore ran for the Senate for Tennessee and won.

Gore became known as a detail-oriented, moderately liberal lawmaker. He became an expert on technology legislation, environmental issues, and arms control. In 1992, Gore's book about ecological issues, *Earth in the Balance*, made the New York Times bestseller lists.

Gore threw his hat into the ring for President in 1988. He won five Southern primaries but was unable to win any Northern states. Returning to the Senate in 1990, he was chosen by Bill Clinton to be his running mate in 1992. The Clinton-Gore ticket beat the incumbent Republicans, Bush and Quayle.

As Vice-President, Al Gore was a big aid to Clinton, due to his experience and knowledge of the ins and outs of Congress. In 1993 Gore cast the deciding vote to pass Clinton's budget. In 1996, Clinton and Gore ran for re-election and decisively beat the Republican team of Bob Dole of Kansas (who ran for VP with Gerald Ford in 1976), and Senator Jack Kemp of New York.

During his second VP term, Gore was accused of improper campaign procedures but was cleared by Attorney General Janet Reno. His popularity was high enough for him to easily triumph in the Democratic Primaries of 2000 over his closest opponent, New York's Bill Bradley. As his running mate he chose Joseph Lieberman from Connecticut.

The Republican team of George W. Bush and his VP Dick Cheney were declared the winners of the 2000 election by the Supreme Court. The race was hotly contested, especially the results from the state of Florida.

Gore handled defeat gracefully and went on to take a teaching position at Columbia University's Graduate School of Journalism. In 2004 he declined to run again. He spoke at the Democratic Convention but generally kept a low profile.

Since then Gore has become a board member at Apple Corp, won a Nobel Peace Prize in 2007 for his film, *An Inconvenient Truth* and its ecological theme, and won a Grammy, Academy Award, Webby, and Emmy for his environmental movie and pursuits.

Alan Naldrett

DICK CHENEY—THE VEEP THE DEVIL FEARS

Richard Bruce Cheney (1941) was the 46th Vice-President, and some thought the most powerful VP ever, having a strong effect on his president, George W. Bush.

Cheney was born in Lincoln, Nebraska to a father who was a soil-conservation agent for the government. The family moved to Casper, Wyoming in 1954, when Cheney was 13. In his high school, he was President of the Senior Class and met his wife Lynne.

Cheney attended Yale University on a scholarship but flunked out due to, as he confessed, "goofing off." He then worked as a utility linesman while earning a bachelor's and master's degree in Political Science from the University of Wyoming. He entered a doctoral program at the University of Wisconsin at Madison that helped him get five student deferments during the Vietnam era.

In 1968 he left school without earning his doctorate. He began working in the office of William Steiger, a Wisconsin Republican, and wrote out his ideas about reorganizing the Office of Economic Opportunity. The paper came to the attention of Donald Rumsfeld, who was President Ford's Chief of Staff. Rumsfeld brought on Cheney as his deputy. When Rumsfeld moved on to become the Secretary of Defense, Cheney became Ford's Chief of Staff from 1975 to 1977.

When Ford lost the election to Jimmy Carter, Cheney went home to Wyoming and ran for their lone House seat. He won the election and served from 1979 to 1989. While in Congress he served as the House Minority Whip and the Chair of the House Republican Conference.

In 1989 he was asked and accepted President George H.W. Bush's invitation to become his Secretary of Defense. He served as head of the Department of Defense for Bush's full term, until 1993. The Desert Storm conflict happened during his tenure.

While the Republicans were out of office, Cheney became the Chairman and CEO of Halliburton Company, from 1995 to 2000. When George W. Bush won the Republican nomination for 2000, Cheney went from heading the committee to find a VP candidate to becoming the VP candidate.

The Cheney-Bush team successfully won a hard-fought election contest against the Gore-Lieberman ticket. Cheney was a leading figure in the Executive branch, helping make decisions as the U.S. suffered through the 9/11 terror attacks, the Afghani war, the Iraq War, and the economic downslide. Cheney had a lot of controversial opinions on combating terrorism, including his belief in the use of torture to elicit information from captives and the practice of the U.S. spying on its own citizens.

The team of Bush and Cheney ran for re-election and beat the Democratic team of John Kerry and VP John Edwards.

Following his stint as Vice-President, Cheney went back to Wyoming, becoming a frequent critic of the Obama Administration. Cheney has been known to suffer at least four heart attacks but has come through each one seemingly without repercussions.

Alan Naldrett

JOE BIDEN—YOUR FAVORITE UNCLE

Joseph Robinette Biden (1942) became the 48th Vice-President when Barack Obama won the 2010 Presidential election. Before that, Biden had been a Senator from Delaware from 1973 to 2009.

Joe Biden was born in Scranton, Pennsylvania and lived there until he was 10 years old, when the family moved to Mayfield, Delaware. He overcame a stutter when he was young by memorizing and reciting long passages of poetry.

Biden went to the University of Delaware where he studied political science and history and graduated in 1965. He went on to the Syracuse University Law School and graduated in 1968. Biden passed the bar and moved to Delaware to begin practicing law. In 1970 he was elected to the New Castle County Council as a Democrat. In 1971, while still a councilman, he started his own law firm.

OBAMA
BIDEN

In 1972 Biden was encouraged by the local Democratic Party members to run for one of the Delaware Senate seats. Come November, with campaign help from the entire family, Biden won in an upset. However, a week before Christmas in 1972, Biden's wife and daughter were killed in a horrific auto accident. His two sons Beau and Hunter were severely injured.

Biden reluctantly began his Senate term, skipping the ceremonial swearing-in ceremony to be with his sons in the hospital. Continually throughout his Senate career, he lived in his Wilmington home and commuted via Amtrak train to Washington each day, so that he could spend more time with his sons.

During his Senate career Biden became Chairman of the Senate Foreign Relations Committee, as well as Chairman of the Senate Judiciary Committee.

In 2008, Democratic Presidential Nominee asked Biden to be his running-mate and Biden agreed. The two won against the Republican team of John McCain and his VP candidate, Governor Sarah Palin of Alaska.

Despite a hostile Republican Congress, the Obama-Biden team managed to pass the nation's first comprehensive health care bill, headed off the nation's bankruptcy, and set in motion lots of other reforms.

In 2012, the Obama-Biden team ran for re-election, successfully beating the team of Mitt Romney and his running mate Paul Ryan.

As the Republican Party won the White House in 2016, Biden became an outspoken critic.

Alan Naldrett

MIKE PENCE—THE MOST TIGHTLY CLENCHED VEEP EVER

Republican Michael Pence (1959), became the 48th Vice-President when Donald Trump was elected President in 2016. Prior to becoming Vice-President, Pence was the Governor of Indiana.

Born in Columbus, Indiana, he attended public schools and then went to Hanover College. After earning a bachelor's degree, Pence attended law school at the Indiana University Robert H. McKinney School of Law, earning a law degree and going into private practice. He unsuccessfully ran for a House seat in 1988 and 1990 and then became a conservative talk radio host from 1994 to 1999. In 2000, he was elected to the House of Representatives, and then was re-elected until 2012, when Pence successfully ran for Governor of Indiana.

In 2016, Trump asked Pence to be his running mate. Pence agreed, and the duo won in 2016, beating the Democratic team of Hillary Clinton.

1988-90   **1992**   **2000**

The 25th Amendment to the U.S. Constitution

Section 1. In case of the removal of the President from office or of his death or resignation, the Vice President shall become President.

Section 2. Whenever there is a vacancy in the office of the Vice President, the President shall nominate a Vice President who shall take office upon confirmation by a majority vote of both Houses of Congress.

Section 3. Whenever the President transmits to the President pro tempore of the Senate and the Speaker of the House of Representatives his written declaration that he is unable to discharge the powers and duties of his office, and until he transmits to them a written declaration to the contrary, such powers and duties shall be discharged by the Vice President as Acting President.

Section 4. Whenever the Vice President and a majority of either the principal officers of the executive departments or of such other body as Congress may by law provide, transmit to the President pro tempore of the Senate and the Speaker of the House of Representatives their written declaration that the President is unable to discharge the powers and duties of his office, the Vice President shall immediately assume the powers and duties of the office as Acting President.

Thereafter, when the President transmits to the President pro tempore of the Senate and the Speaker of the House of Representatives his written declaration that no inability exists, he shall resume the powers and duties of his office unless the Vice President and a majority of either the principal officers of the executive department or of such other body as Congress may by law provide, transmit within four days to the President pro tempore of the Senate and the Speaker of the House of Representatives their written declaration that the President is unable to discharge the powers and duties of his office. Thereupon Congress shall decide the issue, assembling within forty-eight hours for that purpose if not in session. If the Congress, within twenty-one days after receipt of the latter written declaration, or, if Congress is not in session, within twenty-one days after Congress is required to assemble, determines by two-thirds vote of both Houses that the President is unable to discharge the powers and duties of his office, the Vice President shall continue to discharge the same as Acting President; otherwise, the President shall resume the powers and duties of his office.

Tie Breaking Votes by Vice-Presidents

Rank by # of Tie-breaking votes	# of Tie-breaking votes	President of the Senate	Party	Order in Office	Term of office	President(s)
1	31	John C. Calhoun	Democratic-Republican	7	Mar 4, 1825 – Dec 28, 1832	J. Q. Adams / Andrew Jackson
2	29	John Adams	Federalist	1	Apr 21, 1789 – Mar 4, 1797	George Washington
3	19	George Dallas	Democratic	11	Mar 4, 1845 – Mar 4, 1849	James K. Polk
4	18	Schuyler Colfax	Republican	17	Mar 4, 1869 – Mar 4, 1873	Ulysses S. Grant
5	14	George Clinton	Democratic-Republican	4	Mar 4, 1805 – Apr 20, 1812	Thomas Jefferson / James Madison
5	14	Richard M. Johnson	Democratic	9	Mar 4, 1837 – Mar 4, 1841	Martin Van Buren
7	10	John C. Breckinridge	Democratic	14	Mar 4, 1857 – Mar 4, 1861	James Buchanan
8	9	Elbridge Gerry	Democratic-Republican	5	Mar 4, 1813 – Nov 23, 1814	James Madison
8	9	Thomas R. Marshall	Democratic	28	Mar 4, 1913 – Mar 4, 1921	Woodrow Wilson
8	9	Mike Pence	Republican	48	Jan 20, 2017 – present	Donald Trump
11	8	Alben W. Barkley	Democratic	35	Jan 20, 1949 – Jan 20, 1953	Harry S. Truman
11	8	Richard M. Nixon	Republican	36	Jan 20, 1953 – Jan 20, 1961	Dwight D. Eisenhower
11	8	Dick Cheney	Republican	46	Jan 20, 2001 – Jan 20, 2009	George W. Bush
14	7	Hannibal Hamlin	Republican	15	Mar 4, 1861 – Mar 4, 1865	Abraham Lincoln
14	7	George H. W. Bush	Republican	43	Jan 20, 1981 – Jan 20, 1989	Ronald Reagan
16	6	Daniel D. Tompkins	Democratic-Republican	6	Mar 4, 1817 – Mar 4, 1825	James Monroe
16	6	William A. Wheeler	Republican	19	Mar 4, 1877 – Mar 4, 1881	Rutherford B. Hayes
18	4	Martin Van Buren	Democratic	8	Mar 4, 1833 – Mar 4, 1837	Andrew Jackson
18	4	Levi P. Morton	Republican	22	Mar 4, 1889 – Mar 4, 1893	Benjamin Harrison
18	4	James S. Sherman	Republican	27	Mar 4, 1909 – Oct 30, 1912	William H. Taft
18	4	Henry A. Wallace	Democratic	33	Jan 20, 1941 – Jan 20, 1945	Franklin D. Roosevelt
18	4	Hubert H. Humphrey	Democratic	38	Jan 20, 1965 – Jan 20, 1969	Lyndon B. Johnson

18	4	Al Gore	Democratic	45	Jan 20, 1993 – Jan 20, 2001	Bill Clinton
24	3	Thomas Jefferson	Democratic-Republican	2	Mar 4, 1797 – Mar 4, 1801	John Adams
24	3	Aaron Burr	Democratic-Republican	3	Mar 4, 1801 – Mar 4, 1805	Thomas Jefferson
24	3	Millard Fillmore	Whig	12	Mar 4, 1849 – Jul 9, 1850	Zachary Taylor
24	3	Chester A. Arthur	Republican	20	Mar 4, 1881 – Sep 19, 1881	James A. Garfield
24	3	Charles Curtis	Republican	31	Mar 4, 1929 – Mar 4, 1933	Herbert Hoover
24	3	John N. Garner	Democratic	32	Mar 4, 1933 – Jan 20, 1941	Franklin D. Roosevelt
30	2	Adlai Stevenson	Democratic	23	Mar 4, 1893 – Mar 4, 1897	Grover Cleveland
30	2	Charles G. Dawes	Republican	30	Mar 4, 1925 – Mar 4, 1929	Calvin Coolidge
30	2	Spiro T. Agnew	Republican	39	Jan 20, 1969 – Oct 10, 1973	Richard M. Nixon
33	1	Henry Wilson	Republican	18	Mar 4, 1873 – Nov 22, 1875	Ulysses S. Grant
33	1	Garret A. Hobart	Republican	24	Mar 4, 1897 – Nov 21, 1899	William McKinley
33	1	Harry S. Truman	Democratic	34	Jan 20, 1945 – Apr 12, 1945	Franklin D. Roosevelt
33	1	Walter F. Mondale	Democratic	42	Jan 20, 1977 – Jan 20, 1981	Jimmy Carter
37	0	John Tyler	Whig	10	Mar 4, 1841 – Apr 4, 1841	William H. Harrison
37	0	William R. King	Democratic	13	Mar 4, 1853 – Apr 18, 1853	Franklin Pierce
37	0	Andrew Johnson	National Union	16	Mar 4, 1865 – Apr 15, 1865	Abraham Lincoln
37	0	Thomas A. Hendricks	Democratic	21	Mar 4, 1885 – Nov 25, 1885	Grover Cleveland
37	0	Theodore Roosevelt	Republican	25	Mar 4, 1901 – Sep 14, 1901	William McKinley
37	0	Charles W. Fairbanks	Republican	26	Mar 4, 1905 – Mar 4, 1909	Theodore Roosevelt
37	0	Calvin Coolidge	Republican	29	Mar 4, 1921 – Aug 2, 1923	Warren G. Harding
37	0	Lyndon B. Johnson	Democratic	37	Jan 20, 1961 – Nov 22, 1963	John F. Kennedy
37	0	Gerald R. Ford	Republican	40	Dec 6, 1973 – Aug 9, 1974	Richard M. Nixon
37	0	Nelson A. Rockefeller	Republican	41	Dec 19, 1974 – Jan 20, 1977	Gerald Ford
37	0	Dan Quayle	Republican	44	Jan 20, 1989 – Jan 20, 1993	George H. W. Bush
37	0	Joe Biden	Democratic	47	Jan 20, 2009 – Jan 20, 2017	Barack Obama

Courtesy of Wikipedia

Sources

Barzman, Sol (1974). *Madmen and Geniuses: The Vice-Presidents of the United States.* Chicago, IL: Follett Publishing Company.

Coen, Dan (2004). *Second String: Trivia, Facts and Lists about the Vice-Presidency and its Vice-Presidents.* Tarzana, CA: DCD Publishing Books and VicePresidents.com.

Diller, Daniel C. & Robertson, Stephen L. (2005). *The Presidents, First Ladies, and Vice Presidents.* Washington, DC: CQ Press.

Dunlap, Leslie W. (1988). *Our Vice-Presidents and Second Ladies.* Metuchen, NJ: The Scarecrow Press.

Farris, Scott (2012). *Almost President: The Men Who Lost the Race but Changed the Nation.* Guildford, CT: Lyons Press.

Feerick, John D. & Emalie P. (1977). *The First Book of Vice-Presidents of the United States.* New York, NY: Franklin Watts, Inc.

Hallas, Herbert C. (2013). *William Almon Wheeler—Political Star of the North Country.* Albany, New York: State University of New York Press.

Healy, Diana Dixon (1984). *America's Vice-Presidents: Our First Forty-Three Vice-Presidents and How They Got to Be Number Two.* New York, NY: Athenium.

Kelter, Bill, & Shellabarger, Wayne (2008). *Veeps: Profiles in Insignificance.* Marietta, GA: Top Shelf Productions.

Lott, Jeremy (2007). *The Warm Bucket Brigade: The Story of the American Vice-Presidency.* Nashville, TN: Thomas Nelson.

Marshall, Thomas R. (1925). *Recollections of Thomas R. Marshall, Vice-President and Hoosier Philosopher-A Hoosier Salad.* Indianapolis, IN: Bobbs-Merrill Co. Publishers.

Purcell, L. Edward (Ed.) (2001). *Vice-Presidents: A Biographical Dictionary.* New York, NY: Checkmark Books.

Waldrup, Carole Chandler (1996). *The Vice Presidents.* Jefferson, NC: McFarland & Co., Inc.

Wikipedia Contributors (2018). *Focus On: 40 Most Popular Vice-Presidents of the United States.* San Francisco, CA: Focus On.

The United States Vice Presidential Museum in Huntington, Indiana

About the Author

Alan Naldrett is a Michigan historian with an interest in ghost towns, hidden hamlets, and vanished villages, antique autos, the history of auto companies

Alan has had articles printed in journals, magazines and newspapers and has written 14 books so far. He started the first student used record store at Michigan State. He obtained master's Degrees in library and Information Science and Archival Science from Wayne States University in Detroit and has worked as an academic and a medical librarian.

He has played in numerous bands and one of his songs, Red Light Special, hit #26 in Sweden. Some other tunes include "Nice Girls" and "My Job Sux."

BOOKS BY ALAN NALDRETT

Images of America-Chesterfield Township

Forgotten Tales of Michigan's Lower Peninsula (including the Toledo War)

Lost Towns of Eastern Michigan

Lost Car Companies of Detroit

50 States of American Automobiles (A History of the American Auto Industry)

Michigan's Forgotten Celebrities

How Detroit Became the Motor City

Hidden Hamlets and Vanished Villages

Michigan's C. Harold Wills (with Lynn Lyon)

Images of America: New Baltimore (with Rich Gonyeau & Bob Mack)

Images of America: Fraser (with 6 others)

Images of America: Ira Township (with 5 others) Introduction

Michigan's Great Thumb Fires of 1871 and 1881

Guide to the Governors and Lt. Governors of Michigan

Capitalists, Cops & Crooks: The Mayors of Detroit

Official flag of the Vice-President

Made in the USA
Middletown, DE
23 July 2019